PURNELL'S

NATURE ALL AROUND

by

MICHAEL CHINERY

Contents

Published by Purnell Books
Paulton, Bristol, BS18 5LQ
SBN 361 04182 9
Designed and produced by Grisewood and Dempsey Ltd
Grosvenor House, 141-143 Drury Lane, London WC2B 5TG.
© Grisewood & Dempsey Ltd 1978
Printed and bound by Vallardi Industrie Grafiche, Milan

Always keep the strap of your binoculars around your neck, so that you do not drop them. Never look at the sun through binoculars.

Use a stiff-backed note-book, so that you do not need anything to rest on. Most birds can be sketched by drawing two ovals for the head and body and adding the other parts in the right places. Most insects can be sketched on a base of three ovals.

25th May 1977
Dry weather
Bright
Hill Brow Liss
White Eye stripe
on Oak Tree
Long thin beak
White Breast
Tree Creeper Brown Back

LIFE has existed on our planet for hundreds of millions of years. During this vast time plants and animals have evolved or adapted themselves to every possible type of environment or surroundings. Mountaineers see goats and birds on the highest mountains; deep-sea divers see strange fishes and other animals deep down on the sea bed; and polar explorers see huge flocks of penguins on the frozen wastes of Antarctica. But you do not have to be an intrepid explorer to study wildlife, for you are surrounded by it everywhere.

Take a Look
On a country walk you may see ten or fifteen different kinds of trees, thirty kinds of wild flowers, fifteen kinds or species of birds, and innumerable kinds of insects. Even in the middle of a town there is plenty of wildlife for you to see if you look for it. Go into your garden or the street and have a good look around you. Many of the plants that you see will be cultivated ones, grown for food or for the enjoyment of their colours, but look more closely and you will see wild plants – weeds – growing among them. You will also surely see some animals. There will be flies and bees on the flowers, perhaps some caterpillars nibbling the leaves, and perhaps some spiders lurking in their webs. And always there will be birds: singing from their tree- or roof-top perches, soaring in the sky, or swooping down to investigate anything that looks remotely like food. These creatures have all been able to adapt their lives and habits to take advantage of the artificial surroundings created by man.

Another advantage of nature study as a hobby is that you can pursue it at any time – day or night, winter or summer. There is always something to see, and the changing seasons ensure that there is always something new to be found. Even a small garden will continue to yield new and surprising discoveries every year if you keep your eyes open.

Take a Note
The naturalist's most indispensable pieces of equipment are his eyes – and his notebook. Take your notebook wherever you go. If you find a flower, write down the date and the place in which you found it, and make a note of the type of soil if you can. If you see an insect, bird or any other kind of animal, try to record exactly what it is doing: if it is eating something, try to find out what the something is. Do not frighten the animal, but if it goes away you can approach the spot to see if it has left any tooth-marks, droppings, or footprints. Evidence of this kind is just as important to the naturalist as to the detective.

See how many kinds of animals you can find in this picture of a suburban garden. Cultivated plants and artificial habitats such as paths and houses provide food and shelter for a surprisingly large number of animals. Some species, such as the house sparrow are so well adapted to human surroundings that they are never found far from man.

Make notes about the weather when you are recording details of animal behaviour, and if you see large flocks of birds note the direction in which they are flying. In this way you will begin to build up a record of what plants and animals live in your area and you will begin to learn something about their natural history or ecology.

You will not be able to identify everything you see – even the best naturalist cannot identify every flower and insect that he finds – but it helps to learn the names of the commoner flowers and animals that you see. You will gradually pick up other names and, as you learn more about the habits of animals and the habitats of plants, you will become a competent naturalist.

Make a Sketch

Use your field notebook for sketching as well as for making notes. You need not be an artist, but simple sketches can be of great use when you return home and try to identify a bird or some other animal or plant that you have found. Some tips on drawing birds and insects are given at the top of page 8. Always mark the most prominent features, such as bright colour patches, which might help in identification.

Be a Detective

Keep your notebooks from year to year and *use* them. Compare the first dates on which you saw certain flowers or birds in different years. Were the temperatures similar in the two years? Your notes will help you to be a wildlife detective. Make sketches of the footprints left by various animals that you actually see, and when you come across similar footprints elsewhere you will know which animal has recently passed by that spot. Pay attention to the sounds of the countryside as well. Try to learn the songs of the commoner birds of your locality, and learn to recognise the hums and buzzes of different insects.

The Best in Binoculars

Sooner or later you will want a pair of binoculars to help you recognise birds and other animals from a distance. Binoculars are certainly very useful, but you must be careful to choose the right kind for your own purposes. Do not be tempted by the most powerful, for powerful binoculars are heavy to carry. They also have the disadvantage that they may not be able to focus on anything less than about 10 metres away, and so they will not be very useful for watching birds in your garden.

Look at the figures marked on a pair of binoculars, and you will see something like 9×40. This indicates that the binoculars magnify objects nine times and that their objective lenses – the larger of the two pairs of lenses – have a diameter of 40 mm. For general use, binoculars in the region of 8×30 or 9×40 are best, but if you plan to do much bird-watching in dense woodland or in the dusk you would be better with a pair marked 7×50. The larger objective lenses have the advantage of letting in more light. Choose the type of binoculars which best suit your purposes, and then save up to buy the most expensive ones that you can afford. You only buy binoculars once, so buy the best and look after them.

Take a Closer Look

If you are particularly interested in insects or flowers, you will not be able to get very far without a hand lens to magnify some of the important details. There are many different designs, but the most useful is shown on the right. Choose one marked ×10 or perhaps ×15, and you will be surprised how much extra detail you can see with it. A hand lens is easy to lose, so it is not a bad idea to hang it on a cord round your neck.

The Web Watchers

There are several ways of tackling nature study, or ecology, to give it its modern name. You can select a certain area, such as a woodland or a hedgerow, a pond, or even your own garden, and find out as much as possible about the plants and animals that live there. Do not just make lists of what you find, although these can be useful. Try to find out what each organism is doing, why it lives where it does, and how it affects the other members of the community. Try to discover what each animal eats, and whether it is, in turn, eaten by anything else.

You will discover that nearly all the plants and animals in the community are connected in some way by their food or energy chains. Take a fairly simple example from the hedgerow. Any low-growing plant you like to choose will probably be nibbled by slugs and insects. This one kind of plant is thus at the bottom of several or many food chains. Take the slugs as the next link in the chain. These little animals are eaten by shrews, hedgehogs, mice, birds, and several other animals, so the chain is already branching in many directions. Follow the branch from the woodmouse, and you will see that it branches yet again: the mouse may be eaten by an owl or a weasel, or a fox, to give but a few examples. The fox will also eat birds, which might have fed on the slugs and insects which fed on the original plant. There are so many cross-connexions, that it is better to talk of a food or

Although farmers do not like poppies in their fields, the flowers are a splendid sight. Resist the temptation to pick them and other people will have a chance to enjoy them too. There will also be even more next year.

The weather has a great effect on wildlife. Make a simple rain gauge from a tin and a plastic funnel. If the funnel top and the tin are the same diameter you can measure the rainfall directly with a ruler.

energy web than a chain. Fill in as many as you can of the connexions that link the animals and plants in your chosen habitat.

The Specialists

A second approach to nature study, and one which is followed by most young naturalists, is to select one group of plants or animals and study them in depth. Find out everything you can about their structure and their behaviour. Study them in different habitats and see whether they differ from place to place. You could choose grasses or trees, butterflies, snails, or any other group that interests you.

A third approach is to take one single species of plant or animal and find out as much as you can about it. This will, of course, involve learning a lot about other creatures, because nothing lives alone; everything is part of a food web. You will be surprised how many different species are directly involved with the one you select to study.

One quite simple example that you could study is the common dandelion. A really full study would include list-

Seen in detail through a magnifying glass, this common white butterfly (left) appears even more beautiful. The most useful kind of lens is here being used to examine the structure of a small bud (below).

Although few people ever see a fox, it is not a rare animal. It has become so used to human activities now, that it even comes into towns to raid rubbish bins – much easier than chasing rabbits all over the countryside.

ing all the insects that feed on the flowers and leaves, and an investigation of the numbers of seeds produced by the flowers. You could also study the variation in the form of the plant growing under different conditions, because dandelions growing in a lawn look very different from those growing on a lush roadside verge. Try growing some dandelions from seed: how long do they take to flower under different conditions or in different soils? Some biologists spend years studying a single species in this way, and still do not discover everything about it.

Collecting and Conserving

You will obviously want to make a collection of some of the things that you study, and there are many natural objects, such as sea shells, feathers, and owl pellets, that you can collect without harm. But think carefully before you decide to collect living things. Every flower or insect taken from the wild means one less to reproduce itself or to feed another animal. As a naturalist, you will need to collect a few flowers and insects in order to learn something of their structure. Nobody does any harm by sensible collecting, but do not take home six specimens when one will do. Never pick a flower if it is the only one of its kind that you can see, and never dig up any wild flower.

Many wild plants and animals are now rare because people collected too many in the past, or because the fields and woods in which they lived have been destroyed. Some species have actually become extinct. So it is important to look after those that are left and ensure that they do not disappear as well. This is what is meant by nature conservation. Many nature reserves now exist to conserve wildlife. Some are very small and concerned with perhaps just one rare plant, while others are large enough to protect complete communities, such as woodlands or heathlands. People have at last realised how much more enjoyment is to be gained from seeing plants and animals living in their natural surroundings than from seeing collections of dead specimens.

The Garden and its Secret Guests

OUR gardens are designed to provide us with food and pleasure. We grow vegetables and fruit to eat, and we grow flowers to look at. Many other plants as well as various animals find their way into gardens. The garden thus offers many opportunities to study nature, whether you choose the cultivated plants or the uninvited guests.

Some of the animals that come into gardens are pests that damage crops or flowers. The greenfly on the roses are well known pests, as are some of the slugs and caterpillars. Most of the animals, however, are quite harmless. And some, such as bees and ladybirds, are positively useful.

Uninvited plants compete for space with cultivated flowers and vegetables and often smother them. We call these unwanted invaders weeds. Examples include dandelions, chickweeds, and bindweeds. How do these weeds arrive in a neat, tidy garden? If you have ever blown dandelion clocks, you will have a good idea of how some arrive. The wind blows the light, fluffy fruits or seeds into the garden from the fields and roadsides. You have probably come home many times with your socks covered with little burrs. These are the fruits of various plants and they cling to you by means of tiny hooks. If you throw them out into the garden, the seeds inside them will grow into weeds. Many more weed seeds arrive clinging to the coats of animals.

Uninvited Guest List
Make a list of the weeds that grow in your own garden. Draw their leaves and flowers. Try to find out what their fruits and seeds are like and how they find their way into your garden.

If you neglect a garden, the weeds very soon take over. Try to find an abandoned garden or allotment and see how overgrown it is. There are probably no traces of the original plants. They have been crowded out by the tougher weeds. The first weeds to grow up are small, short-lived ones called annuals. These like the disturbed soil of the garden. If they are not removed, they will scatter more seeds in a few weeks. Larger weeds gradually overshadow

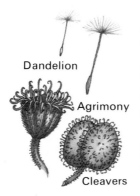

Dandelion

Agrimony

Cleavers

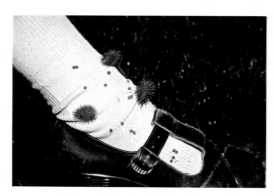

Left: Some common wind- and animal-dispersed fruits.
Right: Your own socks might look like this when you come home from a country walk. The burrs all contain seeds which will grow if you scatter them.
Below: Children enjoy blowing dandelion 'clocks'. Imagine how far a strong wind will blow them.

the smaller ones and crowd them out. These larger weeds live for several years and they are called perennial weeds. They include docks and stinging nettles and woody plants such as brambles. The perennial weeds usually have deep, strong roots and they are difficult to pull up.

Grow Your Own Plants
Most garden plants are grown from seeds, and it is very easy to grow some yourself. If you want to learn about the way in which plants live, and get some fresh food at the same time, these are useful seeds to grow: mustard, cress, lettuce, carrot, spring onion, and various kinds of beans. You can grow these in flower pots or trays of soil indoors and, except for the mustard and cress, you can also grow them out in the garden.

Scatter about 100 mustard or cress seeds on some damp sand or a piece of

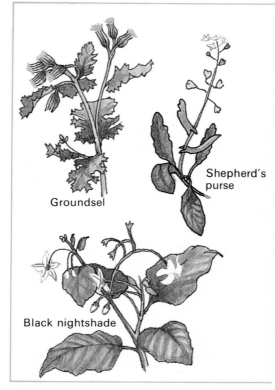

Groundsel

Shepherd's purse

Black nightshade

Ground elder (above) and dock (right) are both difficult weeds to get rid of. Ground elder has a mass of creeping underground stems, while the dock has a long, tough tap root which resists all but the strongest-armed gardeners.

Birds drop quite a lot of seeds in your garden. They eat juicy berries and either spit the seeds out or pass them out with their droppings. Here, a female blackbird is having a meal of hawthorn berries. Elder wild rose, blackberry, cherry, and many other plants may spring up in your garden as a result of birds' activities.

Next time you come home with muddy shoes, scrape some mud off on to a dish of soil that you have baked in the oven to sterilise it. There should be no living seeds in this baked soil.

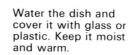

Water the dish and cover it with glass or plastic. Keep it moist and warm.

Ants are very fond of the oily outgrowths on the fruits of dead-nettles. They carry the seeds back to their nests, but drop many on the way, thus scattering the seeds over your garden.

Look at the stems and leaves of stinging nettles with a lens to see the stinging hairs with their poison reservoirs at the base. When you knock off the little cap, the hair sticks into you.

Seeds will soon start to sprout in the dish. These can only have come from the mud that you brought home on your shoes. Think how many more you bring home and drop in the garden.

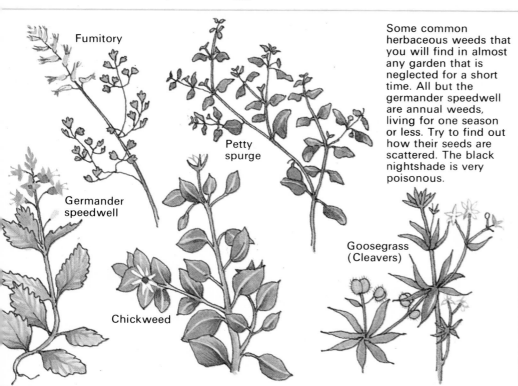

Fumitory

Germander speedwell

Chickweed

Petty spurge

Goosegrass (Cleavers)

Some common herbaceous weeds that you will find in almost any garden that is neglected for a short time. All but the germander speedwell are annual weeds, living for one season or less. Try to find out how their seeds are scattered. The black nightshade is very poisonous.

damp cloth in the bottom of a shallow plastic box. Keep the cloth damp, but not running with water, and the seeds will soon sprout or germinate. How many of the hundred seeds actually sprout? Most of them, probably, because seeds which are sold have to have a good germination rate. A sample is tested before the seeds are sold to make sure that a good proportion of them germinates.

Try growing various kinds of seeds under the same conditions and see how long they take to sprout. You will find that some seeds grow much more quickly than others. For each seed, write down the number of days that pass before the root (radicle) breaks through the seed coat. In the wild, some seeds lie dormant for many years before they germinate. This is why a dense crop of weeds often comes up as soon as the garden has been dug. The

13

Put some broad bean or runner bean seeds in a jam jar lined with blotting paper, and keep the paper moist. Soon the seeds will begin to germinate, with the young root bursting from the seed. No matter which way up the seed lies, the root will always grow downwards. This is clearly essential, because the root has to anchor the plant in the soil and absorb water from it. Soon after the root appears you will see the young shoot come out and begin to grow upwards, unfurling the first leaves as it goes. These start to make food as soon as they reach the light. Before then the seedling depends on food stored in the seed. Plant the seedlings out in the garden when you have watched the early stages of growth.

You can watch a plant's reaction to gravity by taking a small potted plant and putting it on its side. After just a few hours the stem will start to bend upwards. If you could see the root, you would also see that it bends downwards.

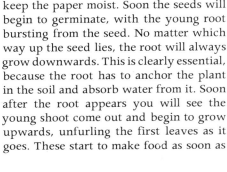

seeds were lying dormant lower down in the soil, just waiting to be brought nearer to the surface.

Grow a few of your seeds in complete darkness, by putting the dish in a cupboard or by covering it with black polythene or aluminium foil. When you look at the seedlings after a week or two you will find them very pale and spindly. It is as if the seedlings have been under the soil all the time, struggling to get up into the light. If you leave them in the light from now on, they will probably recover. The light will enable them to make chlorophyll, the green substance that allows them to make food and grow stronger. If the seedlings are kept in the dark too long, they will use up all the food reserves in the seeds and they will die.

Sow some onion seeds thinly in a small yoghurt pot and keep them warm and moist. When the seedlings have come up and straightened out put the pot on a sunny window sill. You will soon notice that the grass-like seedlings bend over towards the light. All green plants react in this way, so that they get as much light as possible. Light is essential for green plants because it gives them energy to make food. Turn the pot round, and the seedlings will soon straighten up. While they are straight, cover the tops of some of them with little cones of aluminium foil. The uncovered seedlings will soon bend towards the light again, but the covered ones will remain straight. This shows that it is the tip of the plant that

Onion or grass seedlings grow straight up when grown in full light out in the garden.

When the seedlings are lit from one side only, as when they are grown on a window sill, they bend rapidly towards the light. Turn the pot round and the seedlings will bend back again.

Cover the tips of some seedlings with little caps of aluminium foil. These seedlings will not bend towards the light because the tip cannot detect the light.

responds to the light and makes them bend. Plants make similar bending movements in response to gravity.

As well as using packets of seeds, you can grow the seeds that you find in fruit at home. Apples, pears, and plums all provide easily-grown seeds, but it is even more interesting to try some more unusual things, such as oranges or dates. You could also try some of the

CHOICE VEGETABLES

Have you ever wondered exactly what part of the plant you are eating when you have cauliflower? You actually eat the unopened flowers, and this is why the plant is called cauli*flower*. The name simply means 'cabbage flower'. When you eat other vegetables you may be eating leaves, stems, roots, fruits, or seeds. Draw the various vegetables that you see in your garden or in the shops and write down which part we eat in each case. Peas, for example, are seeds, while the celery 'sticks' we eat are the stalks of leaves.

You can have fun by sowing mustard or cress seeds in patterns on a piece of damp cloth. Try writing numbers with them or spelling your name. How long do the seeds take to sprout? You can eat the seedlings in sandwiches or salads when they have grown up sufficiently, but plant a few in the garden to see what the mature plant looks like.

The growing of miniature trees in pots and bowls is called bonsai, and it is widely practised in Japan. Try it yourself with tree seedlings of various kinds. The idea is to keep cutting back the branches until both branches and leaves become dwarfed. You also have to cut the roots regularly as well, but you must ensure that the plants get enough food and moisture. You can use wires to bend and tie the stems into attractive shapes. Be patient, however, because it will take several or many years to produce a miniature tree that looks really old and gnarled. Some of these miniature trees will live for 100 years or more if properly looked after.

nuts that you get at Christmas, but remember to keep the pots in a warm place if you are growing plants that come from warmer countries.

Some of these tree seeds take quite a long time to germinate, so do not throw them away if they have not sprouted in a week or two. And do not expect to get fruit-laden trees straight away, because it takes many years for a seed to grow into a fruit-bearing tree.

New Plants from Old

Not all plants have to be grown from seed. Cut a few twigs from a poplar or willow tree and stick them into some moist soil in a shady part of the garden You will find in a few weeks' time that most of the twigs have sprouted roots and begun to grow. You can do this at any time of year when there are leaves on the twigs. Try it with other trees and shrubs as well. Some 'strike', or take root, more easily than others, but you can improve your chances of success if you buy some rooting powder from the local garden shop. This powder contains chemicals that encourage the cuttings to produce roots.

Gardeners often take cuttings to increase the numbers of trees and shrubs in their gardens. This is much quicker than growing new plants from seeds and, because the cuttings are really only pieces of the parent plants, they grow up exactly like the original plants.

Sometimes, when partly broken branches and twigs reach the ground, they take root and grow. But this is a purely accidental method of reproduction. There are plants, however, which habitually reproduce themselves by producing new parts from old. Strawberry plants, for example, send out runners every year and new plants are formed at the ends of these runners. This kind of reproduction, which does not involve flowers and seeds, is called vegetative reproduction. Make drawings of all the other plants you can find that reproduce in this way. You can start off with the potato, which produces its new plants or tubers under the ground.

Take a few seeds from an orange and plant them in a flower pot in a warm place. They will sprout quite quickly, and if you have a greenhouse or sunny conservatory you may be able to keep the plants until they bear fruit (right).

Gardeners often graft twigs from one kind of apple tree on to the branches of another. With your parents' permission, you could try it yourself if you have a tree. Cut a twig from one tree and cut a notch in it as shown above. Select a twig of the same thickness on your tree and cut it to a wedge shape. Fit the two twigs together and bind them tightly. With luck, they will grow together and you will get two kinds of apples on one tree. The grafted twig retains its own features, and all growth from it will produce its own kind of fruit.

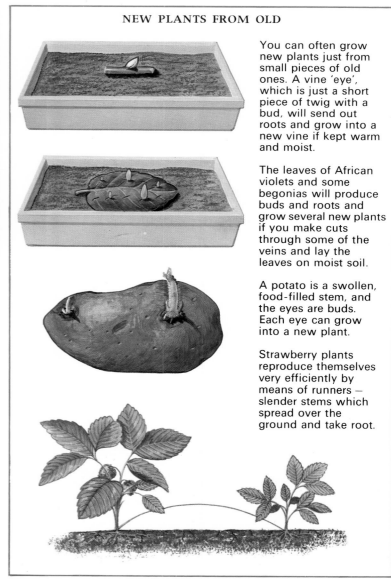

NEW PLANTS FROM OLD

You can often grow new plants just from small pieces of old ones. A vine 'eye', which is just a short piece of twig with a bud, will send out roots and grow into a new vine if kept warm and moist.

The leaves of African violets and some begonias will produce buds and roots and grow several new plants if you make cuts through some of the veins and lay the leaves on moist soil.

A potato is a swollen, food-filled stem, and the eyes are buds. Each eye can grow into a new plant.

Strawberry plants reproduce themselves very efficiently by means of runners — slender stems which spread over the ground and take root.

BIRD BOXES

Hinge

Get an adult to help you make a simple nest-box suitable for tits by cutting up a plank of wood about 2 cm thick, and fitting the pieces together as shown above. The entrance hole should not be more than 30 mm across if you want to keep out the house sparrow. Robins and spotted fly-catchers (right) prefer open-fronted boxes or even simple holes in walls.

15 cm	20 cm	25 cm	20 cm	25 cm	11 cm	20 cm
	25 cm	20 cm	20 cm	25 cm	11 cm	20 cm
	Side	Side	Front	Back	Floor	Lid

The song thrush is a common garden visitor. Snails are its favourite food and it hammers them on to a stone called an 'anvil' until the shells break and it can get at the soft flesh. The hammering can be quite loud at times. Each thrush usually has a favourite stone or anvil, which becomes surrounded by a pile of broken shells.

Bring Birds to Your Garden

House sparrows, blue-tits, and blackbirds can be seen from time to time in even the smallest garden in the heart of a town. You can entice more species to your garden if you put out interesting food for them. It is best to put the food on a special bird table, where cats cannot reach it. Put the table fairly near a window, so that you can watch the birds from indoors.

Make a Bird Table

You can make a simple bird table very easily from a few pieces of wood. The one on the opposite page consists merely of a tray fixed to a slender post. The tray should be about two metres from the ground to prevent cats from leaping on to it, even if this means that you have to stand on a stool to put food on the table. The roof is not really necessary, but it is useful for hanging food on. Leave some gaps around the edge of the tray so that rain water can run away. If you do not have a suitable post, you can hang the feeding tray from a tree or fix it on to a wall.

Vary the Diet

You can put almost any kind of kitchen scraps and other food on your bird table, but remember that not all birds eat the same kinds of food. A look at their beaks will tell you that: there are stout beaks for cracking seeds, slender ones for picking up little insects, and so on (see page 37).

Bread, cake, cheese, bacon rind, suet and cooked potato are all good foods. As well as these put out some seeds and perhaps some sultanas or other fruit. You can buy seed mixtures specially prepared for wild birds. Do not forget to put out some peanuts, though not salted ones, because salt is very bad for birds. Hang the nuts in nets or on strings, and watch the blue-tits and great-tits as they hang on and hammer at the nuts with their beaks.

Split open a coconut if you can get one and hang that up as well, but never give desiccated coconut to birds. When the coconut shells are empty you can fill them with 'bird pudding' – a mixture of seeds and kitchen scraps bound up with melted fat and allowed to set hard. The greater the variety of foods that you give, the greater the number of different kinds of birds you are likely to attract.

Winter is obviously the most important time for feeding wild birds, because there is not so much natural food for them. If you start feeding them, make sure you carry on right through the winter, because the birds will soon come to depend on you. If they do not find food in your garden they may not have the strength to search elsewhere.

Make Your Birds at Home

As well as continuing to feed the birds in spring, you can make them feel even more at home by putting up a few nest-boxes on walls, tree trunks, and garages. As with the bird tables, the nest-boxes must be out of the reach of cats and should not be in the full sun. You can buy ready-made nest-boxes, and even if you are not much of a carpenter, you can make one easily from a single plank of wood. The birds do not mind a few gaps and rough edges. Remember not to keep peering into the nest box to see how the birds are getting on if a pair do move in: this will only upset them and they may desert the nest.

Starling

House sparrows

Suet

Blue-tit attacking
unshelled peanuts

House sparrow

Robin

Chaffinch

House sparrow

Greenfinch

Coal-tit

Song thrush

Blue-tit

Great-tit

Lesser spotted
woodpecker feeding
on 'bird pudding'
rammed into holes
drilled in a small log.

The feeding tray of the bird table should
not be less than about 30 cm square. Do
not put it too far from some sort of cover
because many of the smaller birds do
not like wide open spaces. The insect-
eating birds will readily take cheese and
other fatty foods, but do try to give them
some insects from time to time. You can
buy mealworms or fishermen's maggots
to give to your birds. In frosty weather
you should put out some clean drinking
water for the birds, and change it as
often as you can so that there is nearly
always some ice-free water for them. A
few birds, such as blackbirds and dun-
nocks prefer to feed on the ground, so
put some food at the base of the table.

Blackbird

Dunnock

BUZZ BUZZ BUZZ

Here is a simple experiment that you can carry out to prove that honey bees can see colours and also remember them. Put a white cloth on the lawn, or on a table in the garden, and put a number of pieces of different coloured glass on it. If you cannot get coloured glass, use ordinary glass with different coloured paper under each piece, or even use different coloured saucers. They should all be the same size. Put a drop of honey on the blue glass, and then catch a honey bee. You can catch it

The bumble bee above is busily gathering nectar and pollen. Notice the bulging pollen baskets, which can hold more than half of the bee's own weight of pollen. You can stroke a busy bumble bee without getting stung if you are very gentle. The ladybird eating greenfly below is another valuable friend of the gardener.

Insect Visitors

Many different kinds of insects will visit your garden during the year. You will find them on the plants, on the ground, or sunning themselves on the walls of your house. Walk round your house on a sunny day in spring or summer and see how many you can find: you will probably be surprised at just how many different kinds of flies, bugs, and beetles you find sun-bathing. As I have already pointed out, most of these visitors are quite harmless, and many of them perform a vital function for us by pollinating our flowers. Without bees, flies, butterflies, and several other kinds of insect, we should have no apples or plums, and very few of our other crops would be able to set fruit or seed.

The Pollinators

Next time you are in your garden or park on a sunny day, take a close look at the bees buzzing among the flowers. You will probably see some big furry bumble bees, some smaller honey bees, and several other kinds. Watch them plunging their tongues into the flowers to suck up the sweet nectar, which the honey bees later make into honey. Pansies and many other flowers have bold stripes leading into their throats. What do you think these are for: have you ever seen a bee trying to get into a flower from the wrong direction?

Bees collect pollen as well as nectar from flowers: the pollen clings to their hairy bodies and they periodically comb it off with their legs. Most bees carry pollen home in 'pollen baskets', formed by hairs on their legs. Some of the pollen is accidentally rubbed off on to other flowers that the bee visits, however, and this is the all-important process of pollination. The tiny pollen grains grow down into the centres of the flowers and trigger off the formation of seeds.

Many other insects pollinate flowers while sucking up the nectar. Like bees, they are usually attracted by the scent and the brightly coloured petals. Make a list of the flowers in your garden and write down the kinds of insect that visit each one. You will find that tubular flowers are normally visited only by bees or by butterflies and moths, for only these insects have tongues long enough to reach the nec-

in a tumbler, but it is more fun to try to get it to feed on some honey on a stem. Bring the bee to your experiment and try to get it to feed on the honey there. Put a tiny spot of quick-drying paint on its back. It will fly away after feeding, but it will probably return soon for some more honey, and it will probably bring several more bees with it. When they have flown away again, move the glasses round and replace the honeyed one with a clean blue one of the same colour. The bees will still come back to the blue glass, even though it has no honey.

tar. Snapdragons keep their pollen and nectar hidden inside the flowers, and only bumble bees are strong enough and heavy enough to open the flowers to get at it.

Butterfly Gardening

Everyone likes to see colourful butterflies fluttering about the garden. The best way of encouraging them to visit you is to plant the right kinds of flowers – those with plenty of nectar, like the ones shown at the bottom of the page. Another very useful plant for attracting autumn butterflies is the ice-plant, a fleshy-leaved plant with beautiful heads of pink flowers. But remember that caterpillars do not feed on the same plants. Peacocks, small tortoiseshells, and red admirals all feed on stinging nettles in the caterpillar stage. If you cannot persuade your parents to leave a small clump in a corner of the garden, you may be able to 'cultivate' some in a nearby hedge.

Worrying Wasps

During the late summer hordes of wasps appear in our gardens as if by magic, buzzing greedily around anything

Most moths fly at night, and quite a number come into the house if you leave the lights on and the windows open. They are strongly attracted to bright lights, and entomologists – the people who study insects – use special lamps to trap them. The traps can be opened in the morning to see what moths were flying the previous night. Afterwards they can be released unhurt.

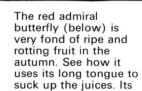

The red admiral butterfly (below) is very fond of ripe and rotting fruit in the autumn. See how it uses its long tongue to suck up the juices. Its

caterpillar (left) feeds on stinging nettle leaves, so you need some stinging nettles around if you want the butterfly to visit you regularly.

Some common garden butterflies and butterfly-attracting flowers include, from left to right: green-veined white on lavender, small tortoiseshell on michaelmas daisy, brimstone on aubretia, peacock on buddleia, and wall brown. The latter butterfly is much more often seen sunning itself on the ground than feeding from flowers.

sweet, from ripe fruit to cakes and jam. These wasps have, in fact, been around the garden for several months, but they have been too busy with their nests to bother us. In spring and early summer you might see, and even hear, wasps scraping wood from sheds and fences. The wood is chewed up by the wasps and used to make a thin paper with which they build their nests. After collecting the wood, the wasps have to collect thousands of small caterpillars and other insects to feed the young wasps in the nest. Many of the insects that they kill are pests, so wasps are not such a nuisance as they seem. Try to ignore them as they buzz around you and they will not hurt you. You are more likely to be stung if you wave your arms about.

The Garden by Night
Take a walk around your garden with a torch at night and you will see quite different animals from those you see in the daytime. The air is cool and moist at night, and many small animals can venture from their hiding places without risk of drying up. They cannot go out in the dry daytime air because they have no waterproof coats to keep their bodies moist. These little creatures include centipedes, millipedes, and woodlice. Look for woodlice on tree trunks and old walls where there are plenty of crevices for them to hide in during the day. Look closely at all the creatures you find. How many pairs of legs can you see on a woodlouse? Perhaps these animals are called by other names in your part of the country. They have many local names: see how many you can discover.

Slugs and snails are abroad at night as well, although you can find them just as easily after a shower of rain in the daytime. Unlike woodlice, slugs and snails are not worried by light. Watch to see what sort of leaves the slugs and snails visit. Do not be surprised if you find that most of them ignore the freshest and greenest plants in the garden: most of them prefer dead leaves.

You can often see where the animals have been by following the silvery trails they leave. These trails are dried ribbons of slime which the animals use to lubricate their paths. They spread the slime from a gland under the head, and then glide smoothly over it. Put a slug or snail into a jam jar and watch the rippling muscular movements which pass along the sole and push it along.

The Goodness of Worms
If you go out on a damp night, late in summer, you may also catch a glimpse of earthworms lying partly out of their burrows. Tread very carefully if you want to get more than a glimpse of them. The animals are easily alarmed by footsteps, and powerful muscles pull them rapidly back into their burrows. The same thing happens if you shine a strong light on to them, so cover your torch with some red plastic. If you keep very still, you may actually see the worms dragging leaves into their burrows, always pulling them in by the tip. Worms do a great deal of good in the garden by burying dead leaves and churning up the soil as they tunnel. In fact, they are the most important of all garden animals.

You can see just how efficiently worms plough the soil by making a simple wormery (see picture). You need two sheets of glass or rigid plastic in a wooden frame which holds them about three centimetres apart.

While handling the worms, feel the tiny bristles on the lower surface. These are used to anchor the worms in their tunnels. The blackbird has a hard job to overcome them when tugging a worm from the ground.

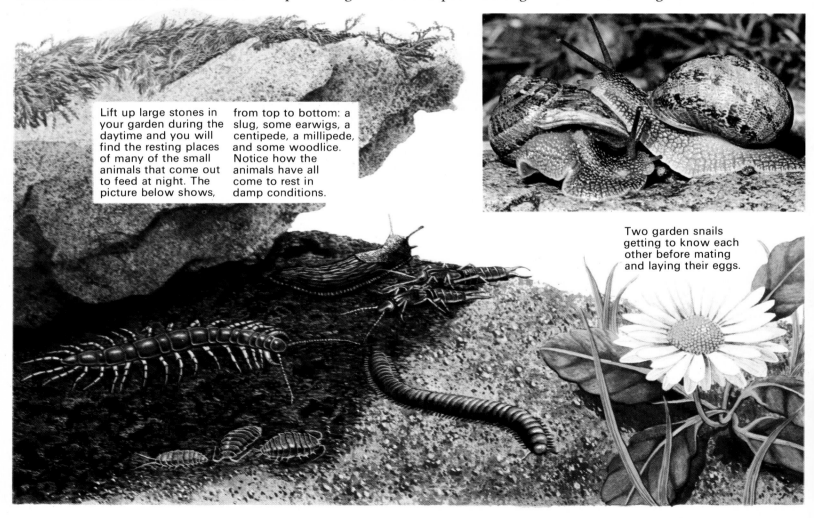

Lift up large stones in your garden during the daytime and you will find the resting places of many of the small animals that come out to feed at night. The picture below shows, from top to bottom: a slug, some earwigs, a centipede, a millipede, and some woodlice. Notice how the animals have all come to rest in damp conditions.

Two garden snails getting to know each other before mating and laying their eggs.

PITFALL TRAPS

You can catch a number of ground-dwelling insects and other animals by sinking jam jars in the ground right up to their rims. The animals scuttle over the ground and fall right into the jars. Ground beetles (seen here) are some of the commonest creatures found in these traps, and you very often find more than one in a trap because the noise of one seems to attract others. Cover each trap with a piece of wood or slate supported on stones just high enough to allow the small animals to creep in. The covers keep out mice and rain.

Insects of the Night

Huge numbers of insects also come out at night, even though they have waterproof coats and need not hide by day. And even though they fly by night, they love the light. Think how many moths and small flies you see around street lights and lighted windows. People who study moths use special light-traps (see page 19) to attract the insects. You will often see bats swooping around street lights as well, for they soon learn where they can get a good meal of insects.

Beetles, earwigs, and many other ground-dwelling insects that hide by day under logs or stones also come out at night. Fast-running ground beetles come out to feed on slugs and other small creatures. Most of them are black but some have beautiful metallic sheens on their bodies. Shine your torch over the garden path and you will see them scuttle away on their long legs. The best way to catch these beetles is to sink a few pitfall traps in your garden (see panel).

A Prickly Visitor

The hedgehog or hedgepig is a regular garden visitor. Worms, beetles, and other small nocturnal animals provide its nightly supper. You will hear hedgehogs much more often than you will see them, for they make a lot of noise as they rummage around for food. The hedgehog is not shy, however, and you can easily track one down with your torch. The hedgehog's prickles, or spines, are really stout stiff hairs, but they protect its body well. If you disturb a hedgehog, it will probably roll up into a ball at first. But quite often it will just sit and watch you and then, the moment that you take your eyes off it, it will slip quietly away. Put down a saucer of bread and milk or kitchen scraps and you may well tempt your visitor back night after night for a good meal. If your visitor is a female, she may well bring her children along with her in late summer.

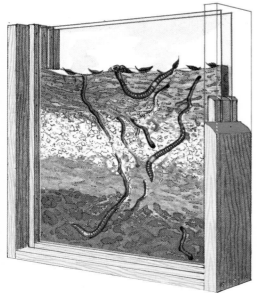

A simple wormery, showing how the worms tunnel through and plough up the layers of soil. Keep the wormery covered when you are not examining it, for earthworms dislike the light. Put a layer of leaves on the top for the worms to eat.

The hedgehog (right) and the wood mouse (below) are both common visitors to the garden, but you are much more likely to see the hedgehog than the mouse. The latter is a very shy animal and does not even like to come out when the moon is shining. When it does come out it may nibble crops and take newly-planted seeds.

Hunting in the Hedgerow

HAVE you ever counted the number of different kinds of trees and shrubs in a hedgerow? Next time you are out for a walk, see how many you can count in a 30-metre stretch. Ignore the climbing bramble or blackberry, and you will get an approximate idea of the hedge's age. Five kinds of woody plants – say ash, field maple, blackthorn, hawthorn, and dogwood – will tell you that the hedge is perhaps 500 years old, while eight kinds of trees and shrubs will suggest an age of about 800 years. This general rule was discovered by Dr Max Hooper, who has been studying hedges as part of his work on nature conservation. You must, of course, take the general appearance of the hedge into consideration if you are trying to estimate its age. A newly planted hedge on a new roadside may contain several species, but it is obviously young.

The History of a Hedge
Hedges came into existence in several ways. Some are the remains of· old woodlands, which were left as boundaries when the woods were cleared for fields and villages. Some hedges simply grew up on the no-man's-land between neighbouring villages, while many others were planted deliberately in the 18th century to enclose fields. These newer hedges are generally much straighter than the old boundary hedges, and they contain fewer species. Many contain little but hawthorn – a very useful hedging plant because of its quick growth and forbidding thorns. It is, in fact, also known as quickthorn. The older hedges may contain some hawthorn, but they will have had time to acquire other species as well. Really old hedges generally contain large stumps or stools, which send up new shoots every time the hedge is cut. Try to find out how old some of your local hedges are.

Lifelines for Wildlife
Vast lengths of hedgerow are now being pulled up to make way for wider roads and bigger fields. This is unfortunate, because the hedgerows, especially the older ones, are very important reserves for wildlife.

Examine a stretch of hedgerow and see how many kinds of plants grow there apart from the basic trees and shrubs that make the hedge. Include all the climbing plants and the smaller species that grow low down in the shelter of the hedge. Do the same plants grow on both sides of the hedge, or do some prefer more shade than others?

Try making a drawing like the one opposite of a section through the hedge with the various plants in their correct positions. Include the grass verge if there is one, and notice how the plants get shorter as you get farther from the hedge. The shorter plants cannot survive in the dense shade at the bottom of the hedge, while the taller species cannot survive the trampling that occurs farther out on the verge.

Blowing in the Wind
Most of our hedgerows are composed of deciduous trees and shrubs, which lose their leaves in the autumn. The hedges thus look very different at different seasons of the year. One of the first plants to come into flower is the hazel, whose bright yellow catkins or lambstails scatter pollen in the slightest breeze.

Look for the tiny female catkins, which look just like ordinary buds with tufts of red hairs on top. These 'hairs' are the stigmas, and the hazel bush cannot produce its delicious nuts until some of the pollen has landed on these stigmas. Because the hazel flowers come out so early – often before the end of January – there are no leaves to get in the way of the wind-blown pollen. See how many other trees you can find that flower before their leaves are fully out. Several grow in the hedgerow.

Flowers Fair and Foul
With no leaves casting a shade, several small plants are able to flower right in the bottom of the hedge early in the spring. They include the lesser celandine and the primrose, and these are followed later by the slightly taller bluebells and stitchworts. These are all basically woodland plants, and their presence in a hedgerow suggests that it was once part of a woodland. Still later

HEDGEROW CLIMBERS

Many weak-stemmed plants, both woody and herbaceous, make use of the hedgerow bushes as supports and they climb or scramble over them to reach the light. Three common climbers are shown above. Ivy (top left) climbs by clinging to tree trunks with tiny roots which grow out from its stems. White bryony (centre) has coiled, spring-like tendrils which coil around the supports, while goosegrass or cleavers (right) clings on with minute hooks which you can see with your lens. Traveller's joy or old man's beard twines its leaf stalks around the twigs. How many other climbers can you find in the hedge. How do they climb?

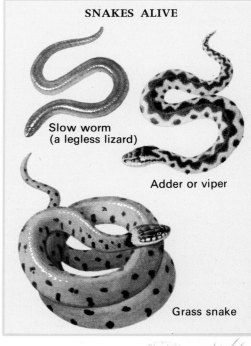

SNAKES ALIVE

Slow worm (a legless lizard)

Adder or viper

Grass snake

1   2

Many elm trees have died from Dutch elm disease in recent years. The disease is caused by a fungus, which blocks the water-carrying tubes and makes the leaves turn yellow and die. The fungus itself is carried from tree to tree by bark beetles which tunnel under the bark.

Lift up some of the loose bark on a dead tree and you will see the radiating tunnels made by the young beetles (below left). Long rows of hedgerow elms have been killed in some parts of the country.

The blackberry (above) climbs by hooking its prickles over the branches. Old man's beard (below) twines its leaf stalks around them.

A section through a country hedgerow, from the grass verge (left) to the dense shrubs of the hedge itself. The plants and animals are:

1. Common daisy
2. Greater plantain
3. Ox-eye daisy
4. Hogweed with hover-flies
5. Goldfinches on thistle
6. Rye grass
7. Lords-and-ladies, showing leaves and fruit
8. False oat grass
9. Tufted vetch
10. Blackthorn
11. Web of garden spider
12. Wild rose
13. Yellowhammer on hawthorn
14. Field maple

The hanging catkins of the hazel (left) consist only of male flowers. The female flowers are the little red-tufted buds. The white dead-nettle (above) is polli-nated by bumble bees, while the lords-and-ladies (right) is pollinated by small flies which are temporarily trapped at the bottom of the spike.

to and from a certain spot in a hedge you can be sure that it has a nest there somewhere. Do not pull the hedge about to find the nest, for this will only make the parent birds desert it, and it is also illegal. You will learn much more by watching the comings and goings of the birds as they gather nest material or food for the nestlings. Notice what sort of food they bring. Watch patiently and you may even see the young birds leaving to make their first shaky flights. They sometimes fall to the ground, but do not be tempted to pick up young birds that you find on the ground: the parents are almost certainly around, waiting to help their youngsters themselves.

In the autumn, when the leaves have fallen from the hedge, you can have a good look at the nest and perhaps even take it down and see exactly what it is

you will see white deadnettles and the beautiful lace-like cow-parsley flower-ing in the hedge.

Watch the many different kinds of insects visiting these flowers to collect pollen and nectar. Whereas the hazel relies on the wind to carry its pollen from flower to flower, these smaller plants with showy petals rely on in-sects to pollinate them.

Look for the strange, pale green flowering spike of the cuckoo-pint or lords-and-ladies in May. A purple club-shaped structure sticks up in the centre and the whole thing has a rather un-pleasant smell. Carefully open a spike and you will probably see lots of tiny flies trapped there. They are attracted by the smell, and they are trapped by a ring of small hairs until they have pollinated the tiny flowers at the bottom of the spike. After pollination, the spike produces its attractive, but poisonous berries.

Autumn Fruits and Falling Leaves
As spring turns into summer, one kind of flower follows another, and then the hedgerow fruits begin to ripen – succu-lent blackberries, rose-hips, haws, and many others. Many of these fruits are poisonous, so stick to the easily recog-nised blackberry if you are hungry. You can use the poisonous ones to make attractive pendants and other decora-tions by making plaster casts of them (see diagram).

The autumn fruits all contain seeds. Their bright colours attract birds which

The robin's pincushion is a common gall on wild roses. It begins to grow in early summer and it may be bright red, orange, or green-ish. There are lots of tiny insects inside it.

scatter the seeds while eating the juicy flesh. Make a list of the kinds of birds that you see eating the various kinds of berries in a hedge. Which are the most popular berries, and which ones are left until last?

While the fruits are ripening and being eaten, notice how the leaves change colour. As autumn presses on, they take on beautiful shades of yellow and red and gradually fall from the branches. Which shrubs lose their leaves first, and which keep theirs the longest?

A Hedgeful of Birds
Birds are the most obvious animal resi-dents of the hedgerow. Watch and listen to them during spring and early sum-mer. If you see a bird flying regularly

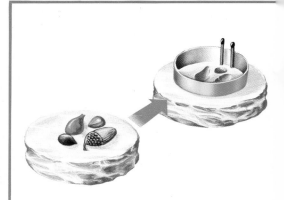

You can make attractive plaster casts of some hedgerow fruits such as hips and haws. Press the fruits into a block of modelling clay to make clear impressions. Surround the impressions with a plastic ring cut from a washing-up liquid bottle.

made of. How many strands of grass, for example, were used, and how many small twigs? You will not do any harm to the birds if you wait until the autumn to look at the nest, because birds nor-mally use their nests just to rear their young and they make new ones each year.

Nightlife in the Hedgerow
The mammals that live in the hedge-bottom are mostly shy creatures. They include hedgehogs, woodmice (see page 21), voles, and shrews. Mice and voles are small rodents and they are largely vegetarians. You can tell voles from mice because they have much more rounded snouts than mice and much smaller ears. Shrews, like hedgehogs, belong to a group of mammals called

insectivores. Although they also look like mice, they have much longer and narrower snouts. You will not normally see any of these animals in action because they usually move about only at night, but you might occasionally find a dead one on the verge.

If you do find one of them lying dead by the hedge, examine it carefully: you might see a pair of black or black and orange beetles working busily around the dead body. These are burying beetles, or sexton beetles, and they actually bury the small corpses by digging the soil out from under them, thus lowering the bodies gradually into the ground. The female beetles then lay their eggs on the buried bodies and the beetle grubs feed on them. The beetles are so good at their work that you will not often find a dead bird or mammal lying about in the countryside.

Spindle fruits open when ripe to reveal the bright red seeds.

Sloes are the fruits of the blackthorn and they are very bitter.

Woody nightshade berries start off green, and pass through an orange stage before growing red and ripe.

Rose hips are full of little pips and irritating hairs.

this is nothing to worry about. It is their way of smelling their surroundings and finding their food.

The Robin's Pincushion
In the summer you may see what look like fluffy red pom-poms growing on the rose bushes in the hedge. These conspicuous growths may be as much as five centimetres across, but few people know what they are. They are commonly called robin's pincushions, but they have nothing to do with robins or any other bird: they are caused by insects. Cut one of these strange growths open with a sharp knife – they are quite woody inside the hairy coating – and you will see lots of little cells, each containing a small white grub. Better still, collect a mature 'pincushion' in the autumn or winter and keep it in a jam jar until the spring. You will be amazed at how many insects emerge from it.

The robin's pincushion is just one of many abnormal plant growths called galls. Most of them are caused when little insects invade a plant and then grow up inside its tissues. The leaves of wild roses often have galls on them that look like little spiked pink peas. Maple trees in the hedge often have their leaves covered with little red pimples, caused by tiny mites. If you want to find lots of different kinds of galls, an oak tree is one of the best places to look for them.

Flyers in the Flowers
From the earliest days of spring to the last days of autumn, you can find vast numbers of insects hopping, crawling,

---

FRUITS FOR FASHION

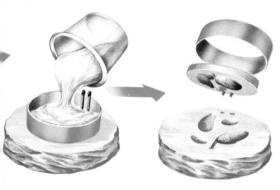

Mix some plaster of Paris with water until the mixture is thick and creamy and then pour it over the block of modelling clay until the plaster in the ring is about 2 cm deep. Make holes for a loop with greased matchsticks.

When the plaster is completely dry, push it carefully out of the ring and peel away the clay. You will have replicas of the original fruits in the middle. Paint them in their natural colours and then varnish the whole disc.

Snakes and Lizards
Grass snakes are quite common in hedgerows, especially damp ones with ditches along one side. You will sometimes see the animals sun-bathing, with their bodies wrapped around the bases of the shrubs. They are easy to recognise by the pale collar just behind the head.

The adder or viper, which is the only poisonous snake in Britain, lives in drier hedges with banks. It can be distinguished from the grass snake by the black zig-zag pattern on its back (see page 22).

A third reptile which you may see is the slow-worm, which is actually a legless lizard with a rather shiny brown body (see page 22). All three animals continually flick out their tongues, but

Bush crickets, such as this speckled bush cricket, are very common in southern hedgerows. They are related to grasshoppers, but they have much longer antennae: compare this insect with the grasshopper on page 40. Notice also the very tiny wings of this bush cricket. The female does not even have these. You will have to search very carefully to find the well-camouflaged speckled bush cricket. The other common hedge-living species is the dark bush cricket, which is slightly easier to find because the males chirp nearly all day in the summer by rubbing their tiny wings together.

and flying about in the hedgerow. Even in winter you can find a few.

Hedge brown or gatekeeper butterflies enjoy sunny hedgerows, especially when the bramble is in flower. Many flies also like to sun themselves on the leaves and lap nectar from the flowers. Flies are particularly fond of the broad, umbrella-like flower heads (umbels) of the hogweed and similar plants. On them you will probably see lots of yellow-and-black insects that look rather like wasps. They are hover-flies – see how they dart away and hover at a distance when you disturb them. Their resemblance to wasps is an example of mimicry: birds are misled into thinking that the flies are wasps and they leave them alone.

Bugs and Beetles

Many beetles also march among the flower heads, including the red or red-and-black soldier and sailor beetles. Because of their colour, these soft-bodied beetles are often called blood-suckers, but they are quite harmless. You can find numerous other attractive beetles by careful searching or by using a sweep-net (see page 32).

You will also find several bugs. These look rather like beetles, but they have a slender, needle-like beak tucked under the head. The beak is used to pierce plants and suck the sap.

Spinning Spiders

The hedgerow is home to thousands of spiders, whose dew-spangled webs are a beautiful sight on autumn mornings. Some of the webs are in the form of domed sheets, with the spiders hanging underneath them. More familiar are the orb-webs, wheel-shaped with the spider often sitting in the middle waiting for its dinner to arrive. See how many webs you can count in a 30-metre stretch of hedgerow, and how many insects you can see in a single web. This simple observation will give you some idea of just how common the spiders are and of the vast numbers of insects they catch and eat.

Select one spider's web in the summer and try to look at it regularly. See how often the spider re-builds its web, and if it always makes the same number of radii or spokes. Does the spider always make a new web in the same place? Try tickling the web with a piece of grass to imitate a trapped fly. The spider may then rush out to investigate.

The nests and eggs of four common hedge-nesting birds: the blackbird (top left), the song thrush (top right), the chaffinch (bottom left), and the long-tailed tit. You must never disturb the nests when they contain eggs or young, and never pull branches aside to get a better view: this may let other animals find the nest and kill the young birds. Do not tell other people where to find birds' nests. In the autumn, when the leaves fall from the hedges, you can take down the nests and see what they are made of. Notice that the song thrush's nest is very similar to that of the blackbird, but that it does not have an inner grass lining. How many kinds of building materials can you find in an *old* nest?

A garden spider (right) sits in its beautifully constructed web. Notice the trapped fly bound with silk.

Look for banded snails (above) on freshly mown verges after rain, and for the large slugs (below) that eat the decaying grass.

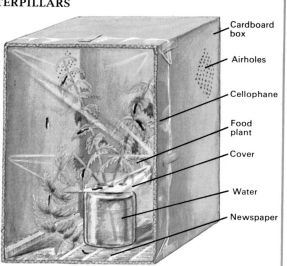

FINDING AND KEEPING CATERPILLARS

You will find many moth caterpillars in the hedgerow. Some, such as the magpie and buff-tip caterpillars, stand out clearly, while others, such as the peppered moth caterpillar, are very well camouflaged. The conspicuous ones are generally protected by irritating hairs or an unpleasant smell. You will obviously have to look harder for the camouflaged ones, but nibbled leaves may give you a clue. You can keep caterpillars in a simple, well-ventilated cage (right). Give them fresh leaves regularly, making sure that each species gets the right kind of leaves. Put some peat and moss into the cage for the caterpillars to burrow in or spin cocoons in when they are ready to turn into chrysalises. Some may take a year to come out as adult moths.

Cardboard box
Airholes
Cellophane
Food plant
Cover
Water
Newspaper

Peppered moth

Lackey moth

Buff ermine moth

Small eggar moth

Buff-tip moth

Magpie moth

Vapourer moth

Drinker moth

Gold-tail moth

Privet hawkmoth

Down to the Woods

WOODS are exciting places to visit at any time of the year. There are trees to climb and leaves to scuffle through, and there is lots of wildlife to see as well – a glimpse of a squirrel, perhaps, or else a herd of deer in full flight through the undergrowth.

What Kind of Wood?

Apart from plantations of conifers which have been planted specifically to provide timber, there are basically two kinds of woodlands: coniferous forests which thrive in the cooler northern lands and deciduous forests which grow in slightly warmer climates. Of course many woods contain trees of

The dominant tree species affects all the other plants through the amount of shade that it casts. Beech trees, for example, cast very dense shade and few plants manage to grow under them. Oaks and ashes cast less shade and you will find several layers of plants beneath them. There is usually a shrub layer consisting of hazel, hawthorn, and a few other species, and you may also find small evergreen trees such as holly, yew, and box. Below the shrubs is the field or herb layer, consisting of ferns and various flowering plants. The latter generally flower early in the year. Why do you think they do this? Look under the field layer for the lowest

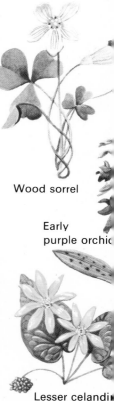

The red squirrel used to be widely distributed through the British Isles, but it is now found mainly in pine woods (right). Notice how little vegetation grows under the pine trees.

Beech

Common oak

Ash

Elm

both kinds. The more interesting woodlands are mixed or deciduous. Because most of the trees drop their leaves for the winter, there is a big difference in the appearance of the woods at different seasons – light and airy in spring before the new leaves open, cool and shady in summer, and a riot of colour as the leaves prepare to fall in the autumn. Even in the winter, the bare trunks and branches reaching up to the grey sky are a majestic sight.

Life in Layers

As well as seasonal changes, notice the distinct 'layers' you find in a deciduous wood. The uppermost layer consists of the mature tree crowns, which form a kind of umbrella or canopy over everything below. In most woodlands there are just one or two major or dominant tree species, so we talk of oak woods, ash woods, beech woods, and so on, according to the most abundant species. See what kinds of trees you can find.

Some common woodland trees (above) and herbaceous plants from the field layer (right).

Mosses (left) form neat cushions on the woodland floor, especially close to the trunks of the trees, where little else can grow. Which side of the trunk do most of the mosses grow on — the drier side or the shadier side?

Wood sorrel

Early purple orchid

The hard fern (right) grows in open woodlands, especially on sandy soils. Unlike most ferns, it bears its spores on special stems in the middle of the plant. Most ferns have spores under the ordinary leaves. Scatter some fern spores on a dish of moist peat and watch them grow first into little green discs and then into new ferns. Keep the dish moist.

Lesser celandine

Blackberry / Bramble

The Blackberry climbs by hooking its prickles over the branches. There are many uses for the brambles, apart from making prickly hedges around fields.

The roots can be cooked & eaten as a vegitable, or roasted to make a kind of coffee. The fruit is delicious & is used for jam, wine & juice, while the stem is used to make rope. It was thought the leaves could help in the ealing of burns & swellings.

The grey squirrel, brought to Britain from North America, makes its home in deciduous woods (left), where it feeds on nuts and other fruits, together with bark, buds and insects. Both kinds of squirrels make ball-shaped nests called dreys in the tree tops.

Larch

Scot's pine

Silver birch

Norway spruce

Bluebell

od anemone

Bugle

mrose

Violet

layer in the woodland community – the mosses and lichens that grow right down on the ground. These are joined by the innumerable toadstools in late summer and autumn (see page 32).

Mapping the Woods
Make a simple map of a small piece of woodland, showing the positions and diameters of the tree trunks and the extent of the tree canopies. You can find this out by pacing out from the trunk in several directions until you are directly under the outermost tips of the branches. Mark on your map the positions of any ferns and flowering plants. Are they close to the trunks, or farther away where they get more light?

The Coniferous Forest
Apart from larches, most cone-bearing trees are evergreens, bearing green leaves throughout the year. These leaves, or needles are able to withstand very low temperatures. The needles

drop and are replaced all the year round, so the floor of the forest is thick with them. Grasses and shrubby plants such as heather and bilberry grow beneath the trees, but there are never as many kinds of plants as there are in a deciduous woodland. In plantations almost nothing else grows because the trees are planted so closely together.

Getting to Know a Tree
If you have no convenient woodland near your home, you can make a study of an individual tree in a park or a hedgerow. You can, of course, make studies of individual trees in the woodlands as well, and it is surprising just how much there is to discover about a single tree. Bark, twigs, buds, leaves, flowers, and fruits can all be examined and collected, and then there are all the animals to be listed; where they live on the tree, what they eat, and so on.

Having selected your tree, the first

HOW OLD?

When a tree has been cut down you can usually count the annual rings in the trunk. These rings represent the wood formed in the trunk in each year of its life. The rings in these ash stumps show that the trunks were about 30 years old when they were cut down, although both had grown up as shoots from a much older stump.

HOW HIGH?

The distance from your eye to the base of the tree trunk is ten times as far as from your eye to the base of the cane (see text), so the tree must be ten times as high as the mark on the cane.

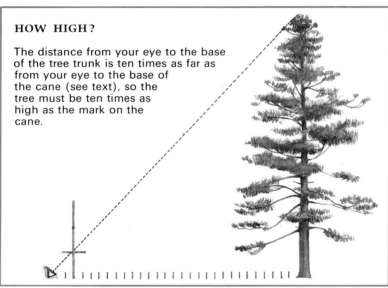

Right: Put some twigs in water and watch the buds open and the leaves gradually unfold. These are the sticky buds of the horse chestnut.

Below: A simple tree recognition chart, with a bark rubbing cut to the shape of the trunk and surrounded by leaves, fruit, and twigs. This chart is of a beech tree.

thing to measure is its height. One simple way of doing this is shown in the diagram above, but you will need a friend to help you. Starting from the base of the tree, you must walk 27 paces in a straight line. Mark the spot and get your friend to stand there with a cane about two metres long. Continuing in the same line, walk another three paces and mark the spot. Get your eye down as close to the ground as possible and look up at the top of the tree. Ask your friend to move a finger up or down the cane until the finger coincides with the top of the tree in your line of sight. The height of the tree will then be ten times the height of the finger on the cane.

Another simple method, again requiring the help of a friend, is to hold a pencil at arm's length and walk backwards or forwards until the pencil appears to be exactly the same size as the tree. Stand still and, still keeping the pencil at arm's length, turn it horizontally so that one end is lined up with the base of the tree. Ask your friend to walk away from the tree until he or she appears to be at the end of the

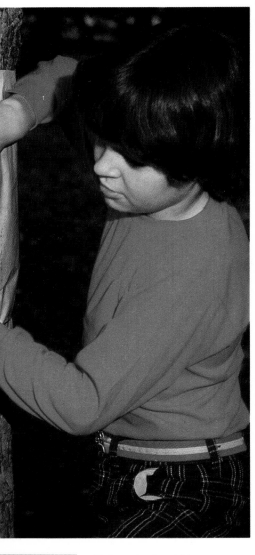

pencil. Measure the distance from your friend to the tree, and this should equal the height of the tree.

Rings of Age
Measure the girth of your tree with a piece of string held round the trunk at a height of 1·5 metres. This can give you a clue to the tree's age. Look for similar sized trees that have been felled, and then count their annual rings to see how old they are (see picture). If your tree is about the same size, it is probably about the same age, even if it is of a different kind. But remember that this is a reliable guide only if the trees are growing in similar conditions. Trees growing under crowded conditions in a wood grow more slowly than trees in a park or a hedgerow. A park tree with a girth of 2·5 metres is likely to be about 100 years old, but a woodland tree with the same girth is more likely to be about 200 years old.

Treasures from Trees
Loose or fallen bark can sometimes be collected from the trees, but you should never strip living bark from a tree because this might easily kill the tree. It is much better to make a collection of

bark patterns by bark rubbing (see picture). Each kind of tree has its own characteristic bark pattern, and a collection of rubbings can be very attractive. Another way of collecting bark patterns is to make plaster casts of the bark, although these casts can be quite bulky. You need some slabs of modelling clay about half a metre square. Hammer them firmly on to the bark so that they take a good impression. Then peel the slabs off carefully and pour plaster of Paris into them at home. When the plaster is set, peel the mould away again and paint the plaster to look like real bark.

Collect twigs from deciduous trees in winter and learn to recognise the trees from their buds. Notice also the scars below the buds. These show where the leaves fell from the twigs. Some of the twigs can be dried and put into a permanent collection, while others can be put into jars of water so that you can watch the buds open and the leaves unfold. Leaves taken from the tree can be pressed and dried in the normal way (see page 38), but you can also make attractive leaf prints and rubbings as shown in the diagrams below.

Many of the woodland trees are pollinated by the wind, but some are

Make a bark rubbing by fixing a piece of thin, but strong paper to the tree trunk and rubbing it firmly with a thick wax crayon. Do not let the paper move when once you have started, and you will get a clear bark pattern on your paper.

Larch cones start off as soft red bodies rather like pine cones, although they are much larger. They take only one season to ripen and scatter their seeds.

The woody pine cone that scatters the seeds is two years old. It starts life as a tiny red cone at the tip of a twig and gradually turns green as the seeds ripen. During its second year it becomes brown and woody. It opens only in dry weather, and you can use an old cone as a kind of weather forecaster.

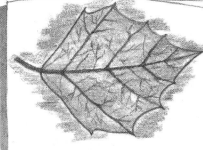

LEAF PRINTS

Make a leaf print by rubbing the back of a leaf lightly with shoe polish or paint (not too wet). Lay the leaf, painted side down, on a clean sheet of paper and cover it with another sheet. Using firm pressure with your hand or perhaps with a rolling pin, rub over the entire area of the leaf. Remove the top sheet of paper and the leaf itself, and you will be left with a clear picture of the veins, transferred by the polish or paint which you rubbed on to the back of the leaf.

Make a leaf rubbing by laying a clean sheet of paper over a flat leaf and rubbing firmly all over the leaf area with a crayon or ordinary pencil. Pay particular attention to the leaf edges, and you will see the leaf pattern gradually appear on your paper.

Make spore prints of toadstools by carefully cutting the ripe caps from the stalks and laying them, gills down, on paper. Cover the caps with a basin to keep out draughts, and leave them for a few hours. Lift the caps up carefully to see the gill pattern 'painted' in spores. Use coloured paper for white-gilled species. If you spray the prints lightly with artists' fixative spray you can keep them permanently.

You can attract moths at night by 'sugaring' tree trunks. You can make a useful mixture by diluting black treacle with beer. Paint a broad streak of the mixture on the tree trunk, and visit it several times during the evening.

A selection of woodland fungi, from left to right (top) are deathcap, stinkhorn, beefsteak, and (bottom) chanterelle, fly agaric and boletus (cep)

visited by insects. If your tree is one of those with colourful or scented flowers that are pollinated by insects, try to find out what kinds the insects are. Press a few flowers in the spring, and collect fruits in the autumn. Dry fruits are easy to keep, but juicy ones are not so easy. You might like to make plaster casts of these for your collection (see page 24).

It is a good idea to mount your bark and leaf rubbings, together with twigs and pressed flowers, on a large sheet of paper to make a chart for each kind of tree. These charts will help you to recognise trees at any time of the year.

Keep a diary for your chosen tree. Write down the dates on which the buds first open if it is a deciduous tree, and the dates on which flowers first appear. The dates of the first fruits and leaf-fall can also be recorded.

New Life from Dead Leaves

Although trees take a lot of food from their leaves before they fall, the dead leaves still contain plenty of goodness and they support a wealth of plant and animal life on the woodland floor. The

plants that rely on them most are toadstools and other fungi that appear mostly during the autumn. For the rest of the year the fungi exist simply as slender threads spreading unseen through the dead leaves. They break down the leaves and absorb food from them. When they have absorbed enough food, neighbouring threads join forces and multiply rapidly to produce the toadstools. If you have a chance to visit a wood on successive days, notice just how quickly the toadstools spring up in the autumn: there might be nothing to see one day, a fine toadstool the next, and a decaying mass only a day or two later. Before decaying, however, the toadstool will have scattered millions of minute spores which will result in new threads.

Look under the caps of a few toadstools and you will see either a sponge-like mass of tiny pores or a lot of radiating gills. The spores are produced in the pores or on the gills, and you can get some idea of how many are produced by cutting off the cap of a toadstool and laying it down on a piece of paper for a few hours: you will get a

A beating tray is made simply from a piece of white or pale-coloured cloth stretched over a simple frame. Hold it under a branch and give the branch a sharp knock with a stick to dislodge the insects and make them fall on to the tray.

The sweep-net is a tough net which you sweep through the grass and other vegetation to collect spiders and insects. The net can be of any design, but it must have reinforced edges to stand up to the tough plants.

The tulgren funnel is a simple device for getting small animals out of soil and dead leaves. Put the soil or leaves on a funnel with a piece of fine wire mesh across it. Shine a light over the top of the material, and the light and heat will drive the animals down through the funnel and into the collecting bottle below.

Life in the Litter

The layer of dead leaves, or leaf litter as it is generally called, contains millions of tiny animals, including springtails, mites, beetles, and little spiders. Many of them chew up the dead leaves and help to return the goodness to the soil, but others, such as the spiders, are carnivorous and they feed on the leaf-eaters. You can see some of these little animals by scattering some leaf litter on a sheet of white paper or by using a tulgren funnel (see picture left).

Forest Insects

In a deciduous wood with plenty of rides and clearings you will find lots of attractive butterflies. From early spring until late in the autumn, you will see them sunning themselves on the leaves and sucking up nectar from the flowers. Some of these woodland butterflies are shown below. See how many more kinds you can find. A great many moths live in the woods as well. The adults spend the daytime resting on leaves and tree trunks. It is well worth-while to search the trunks for them. You will have to look hard, because most of them are incredibly well camouflaged as a protection against hungry birds. Many of them look just like pieces of bark or lichen. Those that rest among the leaves are equally well camouflaged, and some of them even look like birds' droppings.

It is worth 'sugaring' a few trees on the edge of a wood or in a hedgerow one night in the summer. (You will have to persuade an adult to go with you.) Moths will often come to feed on the sugary liquid and you can see how they extend their tongues to lap it up.

Other forest insects can be collected by using a sweep-net and a beating tray, and you will also obtain vast numbers of spiders. Among the insects that you will find will be earwigs, bugs, flies, lacewings, caterpillars, and weevils and other beetles. The weevils can be distinguished from other beetles by their long snouts. They are extremely common on all kinds of plants.

Lacewings, with their delicate green wings and bodies, are both attractive and useful. You may find it hard to believe that such pretty and delicate insects feed voraciously on aphids (greenflies and blackflies).

Prod around in fallen tree trunks and branches to look for beetles and their grubs. This is the natural home of the furniture beetle or woodworm which does so much damage in the house.

spore print showing the pattern of the pores or gills (see picture). Many of the fungi are poisonous, so wash your hands after touching them.

See how many kinds of toadstool you can find in your local woodland. Do not forget the bracket fungi that produce shelf-like growths on living and dead trees. It does not matter if you cannot identify all of the fungi – some are very difficult to name – but try to work out if any of them are particularly associated with one kind of tree. The fly agaric, for example, is usually found only around birch or pine trees. Its bright red cap, dotted with white spots, makes it easy to find.

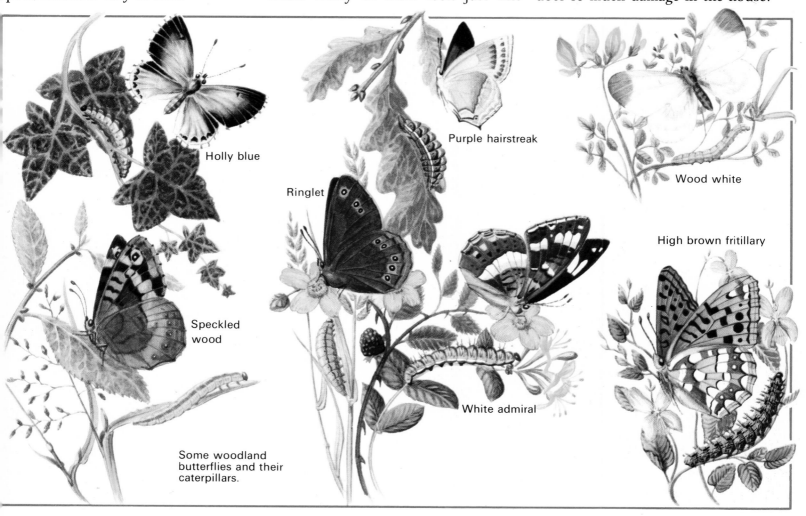

Holly blue

Purple hairstreak

Wood white

Ringlet

High brown fritillary

Speckled wood

White admiral

Some woodland butterflies and their caterpillars.

Hide and See

Lots of mammals live in the woods, but you will not often see them because they are shy and most of them come out only at night. The main exceptions are squirrels. The beautiful red squirrel (page 28) is found mainly in coniferous woodlands, while the grey squirrel, which was brought to Europe from North America, prefers deciduous woods. Scatter some hazel nuts in an area where you know there are squirrels, and then retire to a hiding place to watch the squirrels split the nuts cleanly in two.

Make yourself a simple hide with a few dead branches and pieces of bracken if there is no convenient bush in which to hide. As well as watching squirrels you can use it for watching deer. The best time to watch these animals is at dusk or dawn, but in large forests where they get little disturbance you may see them feeding by day as well. Look for their easily identified footprints (see pictures) so that you get to know the paths they use.

It is a good idea to set up a hide near a pool where the animals drink. You can take a very simple hide with you, consisting of two stout poles and an old dark sheet or blanket with a few peep holes. A camp stool is a good idea if you intend to watch for very long, for you will have to keep very quiet and still.

Deer use their noses as well as their eyes and ears, so try to put your hide well downwind of the track or drinking place they visit.

Night Watch

To watch badgers, foxes and other nocturnal animals, you will need to stay up late at night and you will need a grown-up to go with you to the woods. The badger lives in a large underground home called a set. There are several tunnels leading into the set and the whole area is dotted with heaps of soil removed from the tunnels. Few plants grow on this disturbed soil, and the surrounding trees bear prominent marks where the badgers have been scratching the bark, so you will have little difficulty in recognising a set.

Once found, you can plan your watching. Only one or two entrances may be in use at any one time. To find out which, put some small sticks across the tunnel mouths during the day and go back the next day to see which sticks have been brushed aside. You can then find a suitable watching position for the night. You must be downwind of the set, and preferably a little way up in a tree, and you should be in position before nightfall. Keep very quiet, and use a torch covered with a red filter so that the badgers will not be upset by the light.

Each animal has its own way of dealing with its food, and you can often say what animal has been feeding at a certain place. On the left are four hazel nuts that have been opened by a squirrel (split cleanly in two), a mouse (tooth marks on outside), a vole (toothmarks inside), and a nuthatch (jagged hole).

Voles, squirrels, and other animals, such as rabbits, often gnaw bark and leave characteristic tooth-marks on it. On the right is a tree trunk that has been gnawed by a vole.

Squirrels enjoy the seeds of pine cones, and you can always tell when a squirrel has been at work because it gnaws off each scale near the base, leaving just the central stalk of the cone. The crossbill uses its strange, crossed beak to tear and split the scales to release the seeds.

Left: The fallow deer can be found in woodlands all over the country. Because man has planted such a lot of woodlands during the last century, deer are now more common in Britain than they have been for hundreds of years. There is another reason for their large numbers as well: can you think what it is? (What animals eat the deer?) Do the deer do any damage in the forests?

Right: The tracks of various woodland mammals. Look for these when you are walking in the woods. You will find them mainly on shady rides and paths and around large puddles.

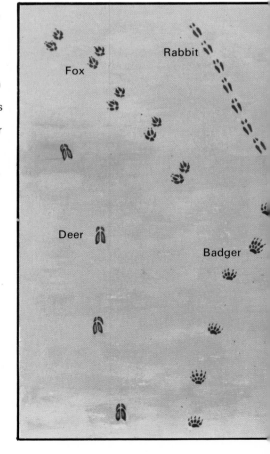

Fox

Rabbit

Deer

Badger

Hedgehog

Squirrel

Dormouse

Badgers (above) are very wary animals and they will not leave their sets if they get the slightest smell of you watching them. Make sure that the wind is blowing from the badgers to you, and keep very quiet if you want to see them.

Three stages in making plaster casts of deer footprints (right). Surround the print with a ring of firm cardboard which must be pressed into the ground. Make sure that there is plenty of room around the print, and then pour in the plaster of Paris, mixed to a thick, creamy state (far right). Wash the bowl out right away, or you will have difficulty in removing the plaster. The plaster in the mould should set in about 15 minutes, but it may take longer on cold, damp days. Don't dig up the cast until you are sure that it has set hard.

While you are watching the badgers, you will see many other animals keeping as quiet as you to avoid being heard by the badgers. To watch foxes, you will need to be extra quiet. A fox's den is easy to find because the fox leaves bones and other rubbish around the entrance. But remember that the fox has sharp ears and a strong nose. It will be aware of you long before you see it and it will keep well out of your way.

Look for the Signs

You will not see many woodland mammals without staying up late or making a lot of preparations, but you can discover their whereabouts and learn quite a lot about their habits by looking for the signs and tracks that they leave. Mice, voles, and squirrels, for example, all have different ways of opening hazel nuts (see page 34), and you can tell which animal has been at work by examining the remains. Tooth-marks on bark are also useful clues, and so are tufts of hair caught on bushes and barbed wire. The animals' droppings, especially if they are fresh, will often tell you where the animals can be found.

The most common signs that you will see if you keep your eyes open are footprints in mud or snow. An expert can look at a set of footprints and tell you many things about the animal that made them – whether it was walking or running, whether it was carrying anything, and so on. Try to learn the footprints of the more common mammals so that you know that 'a badger walked along here recently' or even 'a fox chased a rabbit'. The tracks of some common mammals are shown on page 34. Make a collection of chewed nuts and other feeding signs as well.

Plaster Footprints

As well as collecting chewed nuts and other feeding signs, it is fun to make copies of footprints with plaster of Paris. Choose a nice clear print and surround it with a strip of cardboard pressed firmly into the ground. Mix some plaster with clean water (which you will usually have to take with you), until the mixture is about as thick as treacle, and then pour it carefully into the print. You need a thickness of at least three centimetres. When the plaster is hard, dig the whole lot up and take it home wrapped in newspaper. Wash the mud away under the tap, and

you are left with a plaster cast of the animal's foot. You can keep the cast as it is, with the name written on the plaster, or you can press it firmly into a slab of modelling clay to get a true replica of the print that you found in the wood.

Woodland Songsters

Woodlands, both coniferous and deciduous are full of birds at all times of the year, although you will obviously see different birds at different seasons. Some are with us only during the summer months, while others visit our woodlands only for the winter. See how many birds you can think of that you see only in the summer or the winter.

As with all wildlife, birds have their preferred places within the woodland: pheasants, for example, almost always stay on the ground; wrens keep to the low, dense undergrowth; woodpeckers and tree-creepers stick mainly to the tree trunks; and so on. The birds all have their preferred types of food as well, and their beaks are wonderfully adapted to deal with their different diets. There are slender, insect-picking beaks, tough seed-cracking beaks, sharp flesh-tearing beaks, and so on. Make a list of all the birds that you see in the woodlands. Draw their beaks and note the type of food that they eat. Note also whether they live mainly on the ground, in the undergrowth, or in the tree tops. Where do they make their nests?

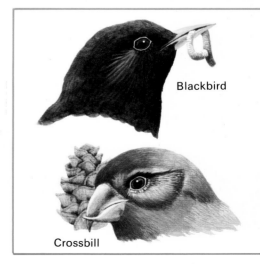

Blackbird

Crossbill

Left: Removing a small jaw bone from an owl pellet. The bones can be arranged on a card, on which you can record details of the size and weight of the pellet. Clean the bones if you want to by soaking them in hydrogen peroxide for an hour or so.

Right: A little owl returning to a tree with a moth in its beak.

FIND FEATHERS

While walking in the woods, you will find feathers from moulting birds. Collect them and mount them in a scrapbook. Try to find out what birds your feathers come from. Never disturb or frighten a bird in order to get a feather.

Below: The heads and beaks of various woodland birds. What do you think each bird eats? The beaks will give you a clue. The nightjar, for example, catches flying insects in its short, but wide beak.

Tree creeper

Nuthatch

Hawfinch

Nightjar

Sparrowhawk

Blue tit

Most birds are active during the daytime and you can observe them quite easily with a pair of binoculars (see page 9). It is more difficult to study owls which are nocturnal. Can you think of any other birds that are active by night?

The common woodland owl is the tawny owl. It spends the day sleeping or resting in a tree, usually perching on a branch very close to the trunk. It is not easy to spot the roosting owl, but the bird often gives away its position by the pile of pellets (see panel) under its regular roosting site.

In Fields and Meadows

Left: An ancient meadow, which has never been ploughed, containing lots of attractive wild flowers. Ploughing and other agricultural operations generally destroy these plants.

Above: A typical mountain valley with enclosed pastures and meadows (light green) and the rough grazings above.

Right: Hay-making in the meadows. An annual cut of hay does not harm the wild flowers as long as they can scatter seeds before the mowing.

LARGE parts of the countryside are covered with grassland, but almost all of this green carpet is artificial, brought about by man and his grazing animals. The land was once covered with forest, and it would become forest again if the farmers stopped mowing the fields or grazing their animals in them. This process of succession to woodland can already be seen on many hillsides from which sheep have been withdrawn in the last few decades. Rabbits used to keep the hillsides open by nibbling off every tree and bush seedling, but when most of the rabbits died from the disease myxomatosis in the 1950's the trees and bushes started to grow up.

There are more than seventy different kinds of grasses that you can find quite commonly, although you will not find them all growing in one place. Some like sandy soils, while others prefer limestone; some are found only in rich meadows, and others grow only

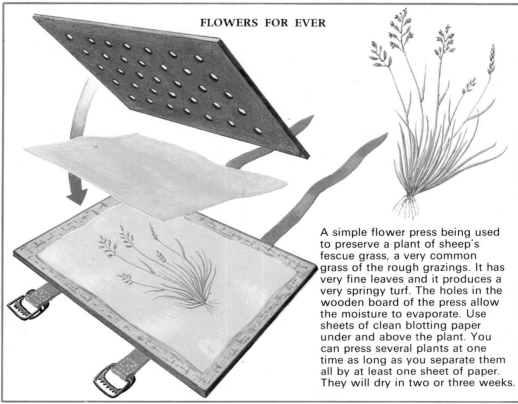

FLOWERS FOR EVER

A simple flower press being used to preserve a plant of sheep's fescue grass, a very common grass of the rough grazings. It has very fine leaves and it produces a very springy turf. The holes in the wooden board of the press allow the moisture to evaporate. Use sheets of clean blotting paper under and above the plant. You can press several plants at one time as long as you separate them all by at least one sheet of paper. They will dry in two or three weeks.

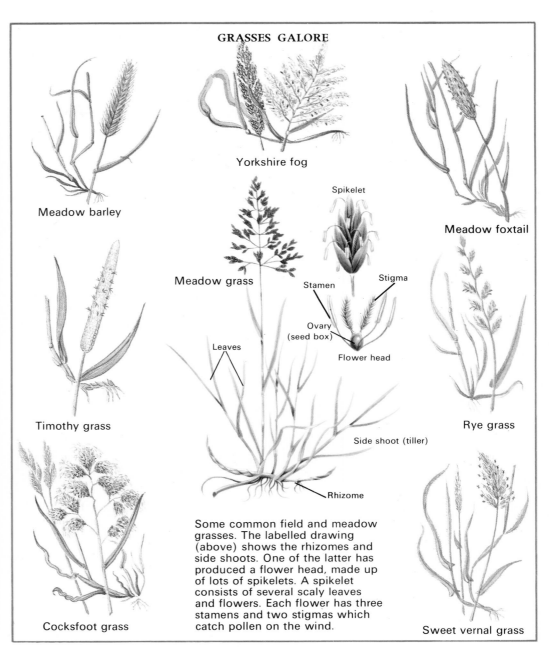

Yorkshire fog

Meadow barley

Meadow foxtail

Spikelet

Meadow grass

Stamen | Stigma

Ovary (seed box)

Flower head

Leaves

Timothy grass

Rye grass

Side shoot (tiller)

Rhizome

Some common field and meadow grasses. The labelled drawing (above) shows the rhizomes and side shoots. One of the latter has produced a flower head, made up of lots of spikelets. A spikelet consists of several scaly leaves and flowers. Each flower has three stamens and two stigmas which catch pollen on the wind.

Cocksfoot grass

Sweet vernal grass

PASTURES AND MEADOWS

Our grasslands can be divided into three main groups according to the way in which they are used or managed. Permanent pastures are the familiar enclosed fields of short grass which are grazed by sheep and cattle for most of the year. They do not contain many kinds of plants other than grasses. Meadows are also grazed, but they are allowed to grow up to produce hay during the summer. Many are ploughed up every few years and re-sown with grass seed to maintain high quality hay crops. Such meadows, also known as leys, contain little apart from grasses and perhaps some clover which is included with the seed mixture. The third type of grassland is rough grazing, which occurs on the higher and steeper hillsides where cultivation is not possible. Unlike the pastures and meadows, the rough grazings are not enclosed and they receive no fertilizer. They often look darker than the enclosed pastures because heather tends to invade them.

on the rough grazings of the hillsides. But they all have the same basic structure. Examine some turf in winter or spring and you will see that each grass plant has a very short stem right down at ground level. There are lots of side shoots springing from the main stems, and they all knit together to form the turf. Only the leaves grow up into the air at this time of the year, for the stems do not start to grow up until summertime, when the grasses start to flower. In heavily grazed areas the flowering stems are all nibbled off, but this does not harm the grasses: they keep on growing by means of their numerous side shoots. Few other plants can survive grazing and trampling in the way that grasses can.

The Grass Flower
Look at the swaying grass stems when they are flowering in June. Some have narrow, cylindrical heads, while others have loose, open heads. Both kinds, however, consist of numerous little sections called spikelets. Each spikelet consists of several little leaf-like parts and each contains one or more simple flowers. There are no petals, scent, or nectar, and the flowers depend on the wind to carry their pollen (see page 22). When the flowers are fully open you can see the pale stamens dangling from the spikelets and scattering their pollen as they are swayed by the breeze. This time of the year is bad for hay-fever sufferers because grass pollen is the main cause of hay-fever and there is often a vast amount of pollen in the air.

Drying and Pressing
The drawings at the top of the page illustrate some of the common grasses that you might find in meadows, on commons, and on roadside verges. The dried flower heads make attractive decorations, but you might also like to

press some of them to make a permanent collection. A simple press is illustrated on page 38, but an old trouser press is even better for dealing with the taller grasses. Collect leaves from the base of the plant as well as the flowering stem, and arrange them neatly on the paper before pressing them. They will dry fairly quickly, and you can then mount them in a scrap book, taking care to name each one if you can. You can, of course, press other leaves and flowers in the same way, but take care when picking flowers. When you pick a flower, it means that it cannot make seeds and new plants. Therefore, collect only the commonest flowers for pressing, and even then take only one or two of each kind.

Buttercups and Daisies

There are, of course, lots of plants in the grasslands apart from the grasses, and it would take several pages just to list them all. A few of the common ones are shown on the opposite page. See how many more you can find growing on the hillsides and roadside verges, as well as in fields and meadows if you can get permission to enter them. Do you find the same flowers on the different kinds of grassland? One simple way to compare the different communities is to peg out an area one metre square and carefully list the different plants that you find in the square. Do this for each kind of grassland. You will probably find that the lightly grazed hillsides have far more kinds of flowering plants on them than heavily grazed areas or ungrazed and unmown verges. Why do you think this is so? Examine heavily trampled areas, such as footpaths, and see what plants are growing there. You will probably find some daisies and plenty of plantains. These plants have flat leaves which hug the ground and which are not damaged by being walked over. Do you find these plants away from the trampled regions as well?

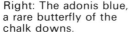

Left: The six-spot burnet moth, with its larva or caterpillar and cocoon. Despite its bright colours and day-flying habits, this insect is definitely a moth: look under the bases of the wings and you will see a stout bristle joining front and back wings together. None of our butterflies has such a bristle.

Right: The adonis blue, a rare butterfly of the chalk downs.

Right: The lesser marsh grasshopper, a common species in moist meadows and other riverside grasslands. The grasshoppers feed entirely on grasses. Some kinds of grasshopper live among long grass, while others prefer short grass with patches of bare ground.

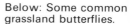

Below: Some common grassland butterflies.

Clouded yellow (a migrant which comes to us from the continent)

Dark green fritillary on knapweed

Chalkhill blue on horseshoe vetch

Grizzled skipper

Small skipper

Small copper

Meadow brown

Small heath

Alive with Animals

Heavily grazed pastures do not support many animals apart from the grazers themselves, because the grass is too short to provide cover and there are few flowers to attract insects. Rough grazings, commons, and hay meadows, however, are positively alive with animals during the summer. Go out into these grasslands and sit quietly among the grasses and you will see all manner of insects hopping about on the plants or flitting about in the air. Poke about in the turf and you may well uncover some runways of one of the commonest grassland mammals – the short-tailed vole. This animal makes narrow tunnels through the matted grass, and if you are between it and its home you may find it rushing towards you. It feeds almost entirely on grass and you may find little heaps of neatly cut grass stems stacked up near its nest. The latter is a ball of grass on or just below the ground.

The weasel is particularly fond of short-tailed voles to eat, so if you sit very still you may be lucky enough to get a glimpse of this lithe little predator streaking through the grass. The kestrel also enjoys a short-tailed vole for dinner, and will hover threateningly overhead, just waiting for a vole to break cover. Wide roadside verges, especially those along the motorways, provide marvellous hunting grounds for the kestrel. Watch how the bird suddenly drops down when it sees something. Does it always come up with a victim?

Do not confuse the kestrel with the other common hovering bird of the grasslands – the skylark. The kestrel is, of course, much larger, but when the birds are high in the sky it is not always easy to identify them: look for the long tail of the kestrel and listen for the sweet song of the skylark, which continues for long periods without a break. The bird usually sings high above its

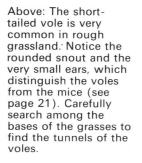

Above: The short-tailed vole is very common in rough grassland. Notice the rounded snout and the very small ears, which distinguish the voles from the mice (see page 21). Carefully search among the bases of the grasses to find the tunnels of the voles.

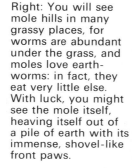

Below: The bee orchid, an attractive flower of many chalk and limestone hillsides. The flower bears a striking resemblance to a bee. Do not pick this rather rare plant.

Right: You will see mole hills in many grassy places, for worms are abundant under the grass, and moles love earthworms: in fact, they eat very little else. With luck, you might see the mole itself, heaving itself out of a pile of earth with its immense, shovel-like front paws.

Below: Some common grassland flowers. Many of our grassland species belong to the pea family.

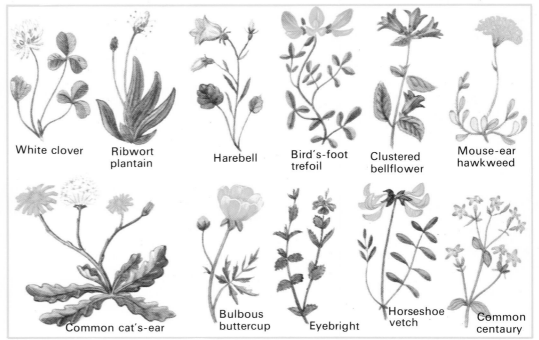

White clover   Ribwort plantain   Harebell   Bird's-foot trefoil   Clustered bellflower   Mouse-ear hawkweed

Common cat's-ear   Bulbous buttercup   Eyebright   Horseshoe vetch   Common centaury

nest, but do not go looking for the nest: it is very well camouflaged and, apart from disturbing the birds, you might easily tread on it by accident.

Beautiful Butterflies

Butterflies abound on the lightly grazed hillsides and meadows where there are plenty of flowers. Several kinds of blue butterflies are found on the chalk and limestone hillsides, where their caterpillars feed on various plants of the pea family. The caterpillars of the meadow brown and the small heath feed on grasses, and so do those of the little skipper butterflies. The lovely purple flowers of the knapweed attract dark green fritillary butterflies and marbled whites. Notice how the butterflies are active only in the sunshine. Most of them stop flying as soon as a cloud hides the sun: can you find where they hide?

Knapweed flowers also attract the brightly coloured burnet moths (see page 40) in the summer. Look for the papery cocoons of these moths on grass stems, and you might actually see a moth dragging itself out and drying its wings.

Fairy Rings

On pastures where cattle and other animals graze you often see rings of mushrooms and other fungi. These 'fairy rings' remain in the same place for year after year, although the toadstools may not appear every year. The rings get larger each year as the underground threads (see page 33) grow outwards. Try to find a fairy ring and see how much it grows in a year. The grass in the centre of the ring is often much greener than that in the rest of the field because the dead fungal threads decay and release food materials for the roots. But a dark green patch of grass does not necessarily indicate a fairy ring: it may simply mark the site of an old cow-pat. Puffballs often form fairy rings. If you find some of these unusual fungi, squeeze an old one and watch how it fires out its spores like a puff of smoke.

Chirping Grasshoppers

From late June onwards the grassland air is filled with the buzzing or chirping of grasshoppers. Try to track down one of these insects by listening to the sound and stalking it very carefully. When you find it, you will see the back legs moving rapidly up and down across the folded wings. This is what

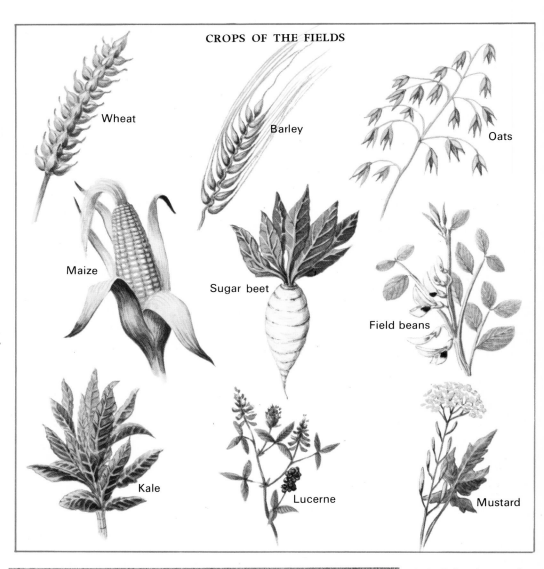

CROPS OF THE FIELDS

Wheat

Barley

Oats

Maize

Sugar beet

Field beans

Kale

Lucerne

Mustard

Left: Fairy-ring toadstools growing in a field. The decaying fungus threads in the middle of the ring help to feed the roots.

Below: Poppies are flowers of disturbed land.

The skylark and its well-camouflaged nest among the grasses.

RABBITS AND HARES

The rabbit and the brown hare are both very common on grassland, and both do quite a lot of damage to crops. They are closely related but the hare is much larger: an adult weighs about 3·5 kg, compared with the rabbit's 2 kg. The hare can also be recognised by its very long, black-tipped ears and by its loping, almost galloping run: the rabbit scuttles along in comparison, and always shows the white underside of its tail. The two animals are also very different in their general habits. The hare is a solitary creature and it does not burrow. Each animal has a home area, but no real home. It rests for much of the day on a flattened patch of grass known as a form. The young hares are born in the form, with a full coat of fur and with their eyes fully open. Look for hares in open country.

Rabbits prefer less open areas, where there are some trees or bushes. They live in groups and they make extensive burrow systems called warrens. Their babies are born in the burrows and are blind and naked to start with. The area around a rabbit warren is very heavily grazed and almost all of the plant cover is removed, making the warren very easy to spot. Ragwort plants, which are poisonous and avoided by rabbits, often spring up around the warrens.

makes the sound. If you could look at a back leg under a microscope you would see a row of tiny pegs. These hit a vein on the wing and produce sound, in much the same way as you can make sounds by running the teeth of a comb over the edge of your finger nail. Only male grasshoppers normally 'sing', and they do it to attract the females. Each species has a different song. How many can you recognise?

Field Crops

Not all the farmer's fields, of course, are used for hay-making or for grazing: farmers grow a lot of other crops as well. Cereals are specially cultivated grasses with large, starch-filled grains. They are important crops in all parts of the world.

In late spring you may see fields completely covered with yellow. These are fields of mustard or oil-seed rape in full flower. The farmer lets the crop go to seed and then harvests it. Mustard seeds are used for making table mustard. You can also grow the seedlings at home for salad. Rape seeds produce useful oil. See how many kinds of crops you can find growing in the fields, and try to find out what they are used for.

Poppies are cornfield weeds, but they are much less common than they used to be because farmers kill them with weedkillers. Drifts of poppies still spring up, however, when fields are deeply ploughed or when the ground is disturbed in other ways. Can you think why this should happen?

The brown hare.

Above: The bright colours of the cinnabar moth caterpillars on the ragwort warn of their unpleasant taste.

Worlds Under the Water

SEEN from a few yards away, a small pond might not look very exciting. A few gnats and dragonflies might be skimming over the surface, but these are nothing compared with the teeming life under the surface. Walk quietly to the water's edge and sit down to watch for a few minutes. You will soon see some of the fascinating inhabitants of the pond.

The first things to catch your eye will probably be the pond skaters, slender little insects that dart rapidly about on the surface of the water. Tufts of water-repellent hairs on their feet keep them on the surface, almost as if the water had a skin. If you look carefully, you will see the little dimples made by the feet, but you will have to keep still because the insects dart away very quickly when disturbed. They use their long middle legs as oars, to row themselves along on the surface, and their back legs as rudders. The front legs are used only to catch other insects for food. A gnat struggling on the surface is very soon attacked and borne off by a skater.

You might also see some shiny black beetles skimming round and round on the surface with the pond skaters. These are whirligig beetles. If you catch one – and this is not easy – look at it with your lens. You will see that it has two eyes on each side, one which

looks out over the surface, and one which looks down into the water.

Coming Up for Air

Every now and then a beetle will rise to the surface and hang there motionless for half a minute or so. Although they live in water, water beetles breathe air, so they have to surface periodically to renew their supplies. The air is carried in the space between the body and the wing covers, rather as a diver carries his air cylinders. Back-swimmers and water boatmen also come up for this purpose. You might see pond snails crawling to the surface by way of plant stems. Having reached the surface, a snail opens the entrance to its lung and blows out a bubble of stale air. It takes in fresh air and goes down again. Because it moves so slowly, it does not use a lot of oxygen and it can stay down for a long time on each refill. The snails can also absorb some oxygen directly from the water. This is especially true of the dark red ramshorn snails, which have the same red colouring matter in their blood as we do. This helps them to absorb oxygen more efficiently, and if you keep some of these snails in a tank with some ordinary pond snails you will see that the latter come up for air much more frequently than the ramshorns.

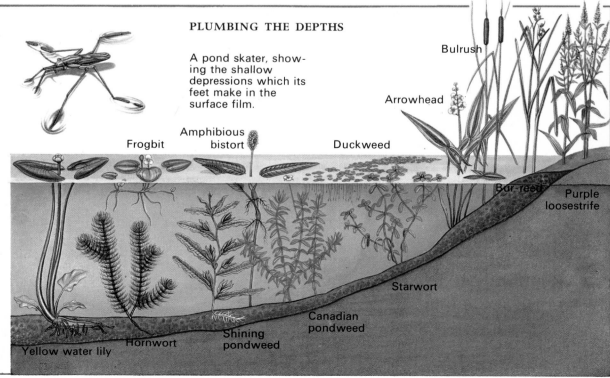

Each kind of pond plant has its preferred depth of water. You can chart the depths at various parts of a pond and draw a diagram like this to show the plants at each depth. Wearing wellingtons, you can paddle in the shallows and measure with a long ruler, but take a stout stick to test the bottom at each step. Deeper parts can be measured with a weighted line and float. Throw the line out, and if the float disappears the pond is deeper than the distance between the weight and the float. Adjust the float's position until it *just* breaks the surface.

PLUMBING THE DEPTHS

A pond skater, showing the shallow depressions which its feet make in the surface film.

Bulrush

Arrowhead

Frogbit

Amphibious bistort

Duckweed

Bur-reed

Purple loosestrife

Starwort

Canadian pondweed

Shining pondweed

Hornwort

Yellow water lily

A PRIVATE POND

You can keep many pond-dwelling creatures at home in a simple glass or plastic aquarium. Do not use a fish bowl because not enough oxygen can dissolve into the water through the small surface. Put some well-washed sand on the bottom and carefully pour in some pond water. Filter it through an old stocking to keep out the debris. Add a few pond plants, weighted down with stones if necessary, and then you can add some animals. Small fishes such as sticklebacks do well in an aquarium, and you can also add caddis worms (see page 47), small water beetles, water boatmen, water lice, and a few water snails. Too many snails will eat all the plants. A single freshwater mussel will help to keep the water clear. Add some water fleas regularly for the fishes to eat, and try to find some hydra as well.

An overgrown pond such as that seen on the left will contain a bewildering assortment of small animals, many of which you can catch in a simple net (below left). Very small animals such as hydra can be examined more closely by putting them into a simple trough made from two pieces of glass and some rubber tubing (right). Use a lens to study them closely. Watch them stretching out their tentacles.

FISHING NET STOCKINGS

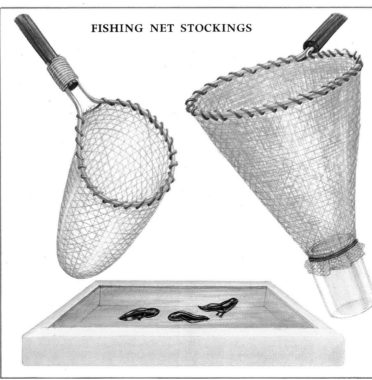

Empty your net into a shallow dish to examine your catch in detail. Very small animals, such as those that float near the surface, are best collected in a plankton net. This is easily made from the foot of an old stocking attached to a stout wire frame about 15 cm across. Remove the toe and tie a small bottle in its place. As the net is drawn through the water, the animals are concentrated in the bottle and easier to deal with. Some are so small that you need a microscope to see them properly.

Under the Surface

A simple net and a jam jar or, better still, a shallow pie dish will show you a great deal more of what lives below the surface of the pond. Draw your net slowly through the water a few times and then empty it into the jar or dish. You will be surprised at the number of small animals you catch. Take your first sample from the surface layers, the next from slightly deeper water, and the third from the bottom layers. You will then see which animals prefer the surface waters, which prefer the middle depths, and which like to live right down on the bottom. It is a good idea to have three or four dishes so that you can compare the different levels side by side. Pull up a few pieces of water weed and put them in a dish as well. You will then see some of the many creatures that spend their time attached to or crawling on the water plants. Put everything back into the pond when you have looked at it, unless you are going to take some animals home for your aquarium.

The caddis fly (right) is a moth-like insect that often comes to lights at night. It spends its early life in water. The larvae of most kinds of caddis flies make neat, portable cases for themselves. Each species makes a case to its own pattern, using small stones, pieces of water plant, and so on (below).

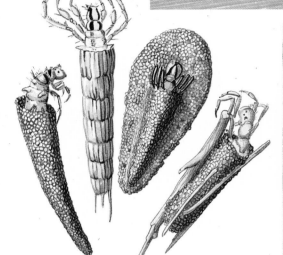

The young damselfly, called a nymph, crawls on the bottom of the pond and catches other small animals for food. It catches them by shooting out its hinged lower jaw, which is armed with spines. When fully grown, the nymph climbs up out of the water and the adult insect (right) breaks out of the nymphal skin.

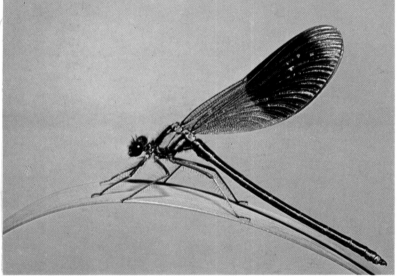

The backswimmer normally swims on its back. If you put it in a glass jar and light it from below it will swim on its front. It always turns its front to the light.

Amazing Transformations

Many insects spend their early lives in water and then develop wings and complete their lives in the air. The dragonflies and the more slender damselflies are good examples. The water-dwelling nymphs gradually acquire the adult features, and you can see the wings developing on their backs. When they are ready, the nymphs climb up into the air and the beautiful adult insects burst out of the nymphal skins. Mayflies and stoneflies have similar life histories.

Caddis flies go through a chrysalis stage in their development. The larvae of many kinds build elaborate cases of stones or pieces of plant in which to live. Each species makes its case to a specific pattern, and you can collect quite a number of different kinds from the bottom of a pond or stream. Using a paint brush or a match stick, gently poke one or two of the larvae at the hind end and make them come out of their cases. The softness of their bodies will show you why they need protection inside the cases. Put the naked larvae into a small dish with some pond water and the right kinds of building materials and watch how they set about making new cases. It is amazing how they fit the pieces together so neatly. The insects pupate inside their cases and then swim to the surface as adults.

Frogs also undergo some striking transformations as they grow up. Collect a little frogspawn in the spring and keep it in an aquarium or a bowl of pond water so that you can watch the tadpoles hatch and grow up. Add some pond weed from time to time, and give the tadpoles some small pieces of meat or fish food when they get larger. Put a small log or rock in the container for them to hop on to when they turn into frogs, but be ready to take the animals back to their pond as soon as they do. Frogs are not nearly as common as they used to be, largely because so may ponds are being drained or polluted.

INVASION BY REEDS

A pond or lake does not stay the same for year after year. Mud and decaying plants accumulate on the bottom, and the reeds growing around the edge gradually creep in towards the middle as the water gets shallower. Unless the pond is regularly cleaned, it will gradually be converted into a reed swamp without any open water, and it will eventually be transformed into woodland. This process is called succession. Study it in your pond.

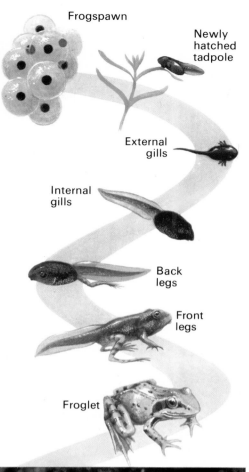

Frogspawn

Newly hatched tadpole

External gills

Internal gills

Back legs

Front legs

Froglet

How about encouraging these interesting animals by making a pond in your garden?

Birds of the Waterside

Ponds and streams provide homes and hunting grounds for many kinds of birds, ranging from majestic swans to little dippers and wagtails that catch insects at the water's edge. The dipper, which frequents upland streams, even walks under the water to search for caddis larvae and other grubs. One of the commonest of the waterside birds is the moorhen, a shy black bird, somewhat smaller than a chicken, with a red beak. It swims very jerkily over the water and scurries rapidly for the cover of the reeds when disturbed. Look for the bird's narrow, four-toed footprints in the mud at the edge of the pond. Prints with lobes along the toes are those of the coot, another common species which has black plumage and a white forehead. What other kinds of birds do you see on and around lakes and ponds? What do they all feed on?

The common frog (right) and some of the stages in its life history (above right). The animal takes about three months to change from frogspawn (eggs) to miniature frog, but it then takes a further three or four years to grow up properly. The newt (above) and the toad have similar life histories, but the newt lays its eggs singly, while the common toad lays its eggs in long strings of jelly. The common toad looks quite like the frog, but its skin is much bumpier.

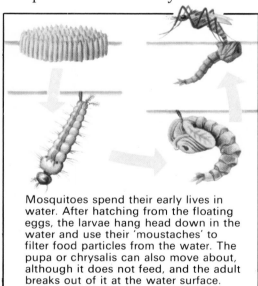

Mosquitoes spend their early lives in water. After hatching from the floating eggs, the larvae hang head down in the water and use their 'moustaches' to filter food particles from the water. The pupa or chrysalis can also move about, although it does not feed, and the adult breaks out of it at the water surface.

Up and Down the River

Many of the plants and animals that you find in ponds also live in rivers, but only in certain stretches of the rivers where the current is not too strong and where there is plenty of vegetation along the edges. The upper reaches of a river are generally too fast-flowing for the pond creatures. You will find quite different animals in these fast-flowing waters. The lowest reaches, which are affected by the tides and the salty water of the sea, also have their own plants and animals. A selection of common river plants and animals, from headstream to estuary, is shown on the next page.

DIVING SUITS

Aquatic insects and many pond snails once lived on land, and they still have to breathe air. Most water beetles (bottom left) and pond snails (top left) behave rather like frogmen: they take an air supply down with them and come up to renew it every now and then. The water scorpion (top right) and the rat-tailed maggot (bottom right), which is the grub of a hover-fly, behave more like old-fashioned deep-sea divers: they have tubes which carry air down from the surface.

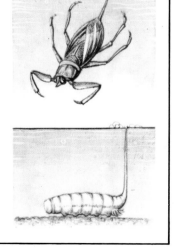

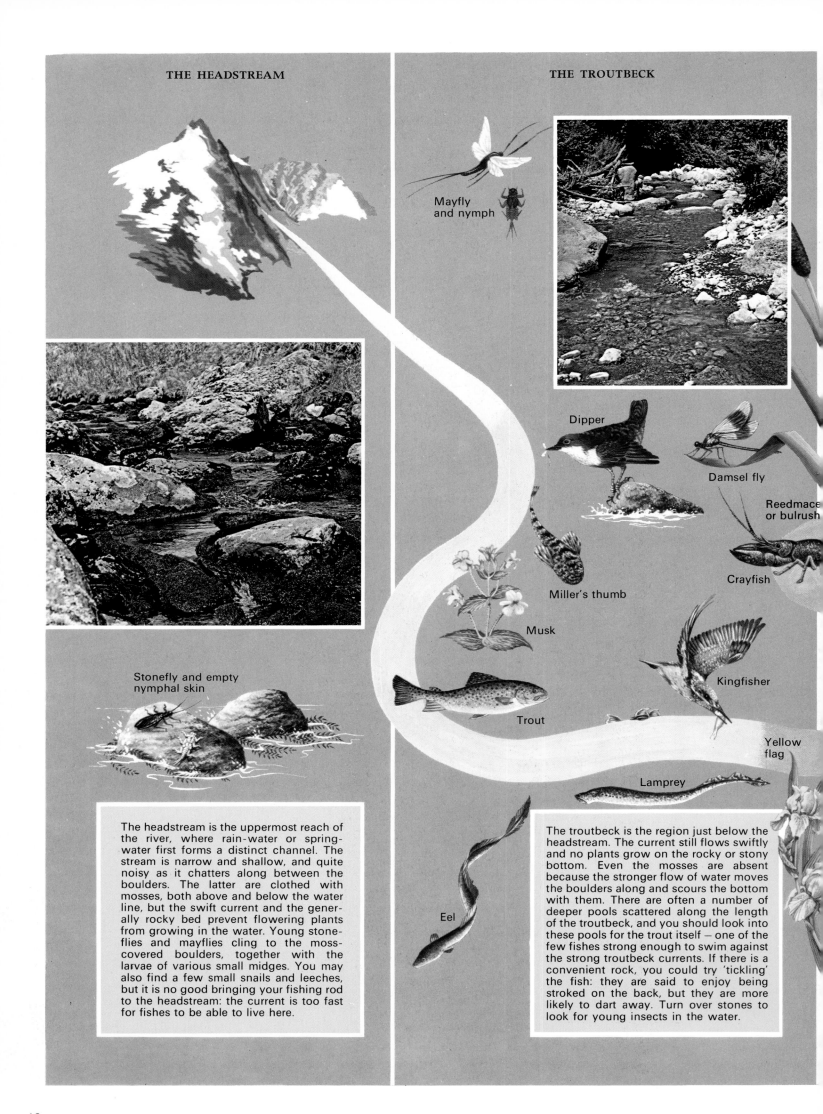

THE HEADSTREAM

THE TROUTBECK

Mayfly and nymph

Dipper

Damsel fly

Reedmace or bulrush

Crayfish

Miller's thumb

Musk

Kingfisher

Trout

Yellow flag

Lamprey

Stonefly and empty nymphal skin

Eel

The headstream is the uppermost reach of the river, where rain-water or spring-water first forms a distinct channel. The stream is narrow and shallow, and quite noisy as it chatters along between the boulders. The latter are clothed with mosses, both above and below the water line, but the swift current and the generally rocky bed prevent flowering plants from growing in the water. Young stone-flies and mayflies cling to the moss-covered boulders, together with the larvae of various small midges. You may also find a few small snails and leeches, but it is no good bringing your fishing rod to the headstream: the current is too fast for fishes to be able to live here.

The troutbeck is the region just below the headstream. The current still flows swiftly and no plants grow on the rocky or stony bottom. Even the mosses are absent because the stronger flow of water moves the boulders along and scours the bottom with them. There are often a number of deeper pools scattered along the length of the troutbeck, and you should look into these pools for the trout itself — one of the few fishes strong enough to swim against the strong troutbeck currents. If there is a convenient rock, you could try 'tickling' the fish: they are said to enjoy being stroked on the back, but they are more likely to dart away. Turn over stones to look for young insects in the water.

THE MINNOW REACH

Mayfly

Bur-reed

Grayling

Caddis cases

Caddis fly
on brooklime

Minnows

Purple
loosestrife

Moorhen
in reed nest

Below the troutbeck the stream broadens out to form the minnow reach. The current is slower and gravel banks build up, allowing water crowfoot and other plants to grow in the water. Several other plants, including musk, spring up on the edges. Minnows, trout, grayling, eels, and salmon are all found here. The kingfisher makes a good living plucking them from the water in its spectacular dives. Dragonflies and caddis flies are abundant. Use your pond net to see how many creatures you can find living in the stream.

THE LOWLAND REACH

Greater
pond snail

Roach

Heron

Perch

Water lily

Pike

The lowland reach is very similar to the pond in its animal and plant inhabitants because the current is very slow, especially at the edges where the mud builds up and reeds and other plants grow. Moorhens and other birds nest among the reeds and there are many fishes in the water. The heron stalks in the shallows and can be sure of a good meal. Use your pond net and plankton net here, but take care not to damage the bank or the waterside vegetation, and don't fall in!

THE ESTUARINE REACH

Sea aster

Flounder

The estuarine reach is the lowest stretch of the river, where the rise and fall of the tide are clearly seen and where there is some mixing of fresh and salt water. Mud banks, often covered with slimy green algae, are exposed at low tide and there are often wide expanses of flat salt marsh covered with sea lavender and dotted with salty pools. Sea asters grow along the banks, while the commonest fish in the water is the flounder.

On the Borders of the Sea

CONDITIONS along the edge of the sea are always changing as the tides sweep in and out twice every day. The shore may be baked by the sun in the morning, and completely covered by the sea in the afternoon. But a surprising number of plants and animals manage to live on the shore, and you can always find something to interest you.

Rocks or Sand?

If you visit the seaside in various parts of the country, you will soon realise that there are several different kinds of seashores. Exposed coastlines where the land consists of very hard rock have rugged cliffs with rocky platforms below them. There may be some sand right at the lowest part of the shore, but most of the shore is rocky. The more sheltered coasts tend to have sandy beaches, for they are protected from the fury of the waves and the sand gradually builds up. Shingle beaches are formed on some exposed coasts, while muddy beaches are characteristic of river mouths.

Each kind of shore has its particular kinds of inhabitants, although the shingle beach supports very little life: the shifting stones would soon crush any animals living among them.

Strand Lines on the Sand

Look at a sandy beach when the tide is out and you might think there is no wildlife to interest you apart from a few gulls and other sea-birds prodding about in the sand. But look more closely, and you will begin to see quite a lot. Look at the strand lines – the lines of debris that mark the high tide level. Keeping a careful look-out for lumps of oil and broken glass, which are all too common on beaches today, turn over a few pieces of wood and seaweed. You will see hundreds of tiny creatures leaping about. These are sand-hoppers, and it is these animals that the sea birds are searching for as they probe along the strand lines.

Examine some of the pieces of wood and you may find that some of them are riddled with little holes. These will

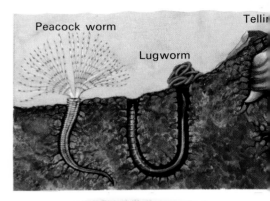

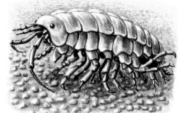

Below: Black-headed gulls and an oyster-catcher search for food along the strand line on a sandy beach. Gulls will eat almost any animal material, including sandhoppers (above), but the oystercatcher is more fussy. It will eat the sandhoppers, but otherwise prefers cockles and other molluscs.

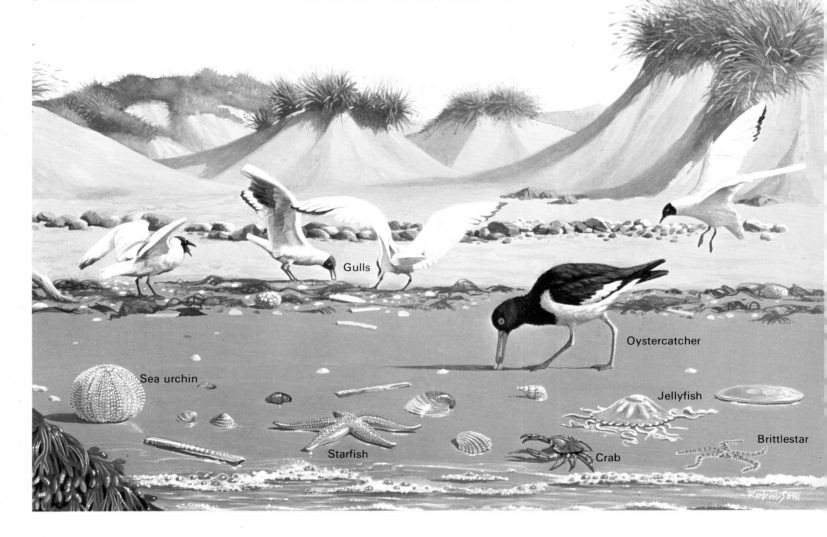

Tube-worms

Ragworm

Many burrowing animals live on sea shores of fine sand and mud. The peacock worm filters food from the water; the lugworm swallows mud and digests food from it; the tellin sucks up food like a vacuum cleaner; and the ragworm takes food with its tentacles.

A starfish pulling a cockle open with its powerful suckers or tube feet in order to get at the meat inside.

have been made either by gribbles, which are little woodlouse-like animals, or by shipworms. The latter are strange bivalve molluscs which use their little shells as drills to bore into wood, in much the same way as the piddock bores into rocks (see page 53). The shipworm eats the wood as it tunnels along, which made it a serious problem when ships were made of wood. Use a sharp knife very carefully to shave away part of the wood and you may find shipworm shells, or even some live gribbles. Thoroughly dried and polished, these hole-riddled pieces of wood make attractive paper weights. Old roots and other pieces of driftwood also make attractive decorations if you find pieces with strange shapes.

Shore Treasures

Sea shells are very common on strand lines and good specimens are well worth collecting (see page 52). Try to find complete bivalve shells, so that you can see how the two halves hinge together. Notice the scars inside the shells, showing where the powerful closing muscles were attached. The oval, white cuttlebones from cuttlefish are common as well: take some home, if you have a chicken or canary, but

wash the salt off first. You will also find crab and sea urchin shells, the spongy egg cases of the whelk, and horny mermaid's purses, which are the egg cases of skates and dogfishes. Jelly-fishes may be washed up on the shore as well, but be careful with them as some can still sting when they are dead. The common jellyfish with the four purple rings in the centre is harmless.

You might find starfishes cast up on the beach. Many will be dead, but some may still be alive. Put them into a bucket of sea water and let them recover. Turn one over and see the numerous little suckers on the under-sides of the arms. The animal drags it-self along with these, and also uses them to pull open cockles and other bivalves. Starfishes have a wonderful ability to replace parts which have been bitten off by fishes or gulls, and you often see a starfish with one arm much shorter than the others: the little arm is the new one being grown.

Going Fishing

Move farther down the beach from the strand line and look for little worm casts or depressions in the sand near the water's edge. These are a sign that lugworms and bivalves are burrowing beneath the surface. Try to dig them up to look at them. Take a shrimping net into the shallow water and push it gently along the surface of the sand. As well as shrimps, you may catch a number of small fishes, but watch out for the weever fish. This fish has poisonous spines and can give you a very painful wound. It is as well to wear some old plimsolls when paddling in water where it lives.

Seaweed Zones

One of the first things that you will notice if you visit a rocky shore when the tide is out is that the various kinds of seaweeds are arranged in fairly distinct zones. Green seaweeds, such as the long ribbons of sea grass (*Enteromorpha*), occupy the highest zones, for they can withstand the greatest exposure to air and to rainwater. Below them come the various kinds of brown seaweeds, such as bladder wrack and knotted wrack. These brown sea-weeds are also arranged in zones, with the very long kelps and oarweeds growing in the lowest zone round about low tide level. Red seaweeds cannot survive much exposure to the

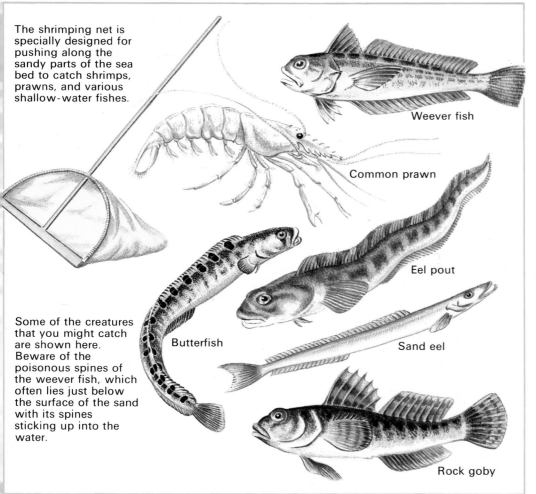

The shrimping net is specially designed for pushing along the sandy parts of the sea bed to catch shrimps, prawns, and various shallow-water fishes.

Some of the creatures that you might catch are shown here. Beware of the poisonous spines of the weever fish, which often lies just below the surface of the sand with its spines sticking up into the water.

Weever fish

Common prawn

Eel pout

Butterfish

Sand eel

Rock goby

air and so are found below low tide level or else in rock pools. See how many different kinds of seaweed you can find.

Steadfast Shells

Search carefully among the seaweeds and you will find plenty of periwinkles, many of them with bright yellow shells, and lots of attractive top-shells as well. The latter get their name because they are shaped just like a small spinning top. There will be lots of mussels, too, with their dark blue shells firmly attached to the rocks by means of tufts of strong threads. The shells are often so tightly packed that you cannot see the rock between them, but they never grow very large when they are so crowded.

You will see plenty of common limpets, with their conical shells pulled tightly down against the rocks. Try to pull one away and you will find it just about impossible: the suction power of a limpet's foot is amazing. But

Tents, Tubes and Blobs

The conical 'tents' of acorn barnacles are sometimes so densely packed that the rocks look quite white with them. Barnacles are crustaceans – relatives of the shrimps and crabs – and they spend quite a long time floating freely in the water before settling down and attaching themselves to the rocks. The chalky plates from which the shell is made can move a little. Find some barnacles on a stone or a shell and put them into a bowl of sea water: you will see the shells open and the barnacle will start to 'comb' the water for food with its feathery legs. Like seaweeds, barnacles occupy a definite zone on the shore. If you are staying by the sea, you can watch the rise and fall of the tides and work out how many hours the barnacles are covered and exposed each day. They cannot get enough food if they are out of water for too long.

Other animals that you might easily miss among the seaweeds and rocks are tube-worms. These secrete coiled tubes of limestone around themselves

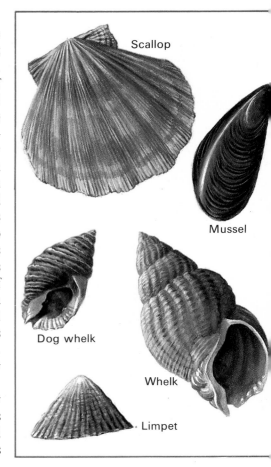

Scallop

Mussel

Dog whelk

Whelk

Limpet

The common gull finds plenty of food among the seaweeds when the tide goes out. Here it has plucked a small crab from among the wrack seaweeds.

"NOW YOU SEE ME, NOW YOU DON'T"

Search for some chameleon prawns in a rock pool, or use your shrimping net to catch some if the bottom is not too rocky. They will be pale in colour if the pool has a sandy bottom, and darker if it is a weedy pool. Put the pale prawns into a bucket of sea water with some dark seaweeds on the bottom and watch the prawns change

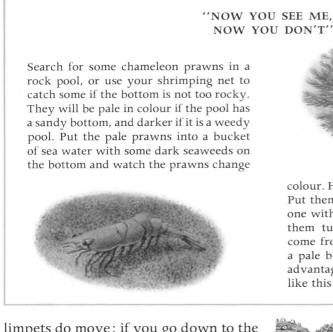

colour. How long do they take to go dark? Put them into a pale coloured bucket (or one with sand on the bottom) and watch them turn pale again. If your prawns come from a weedy pool, put them into a pale bucket to start with. What is the advantage in being able to change colour like this?

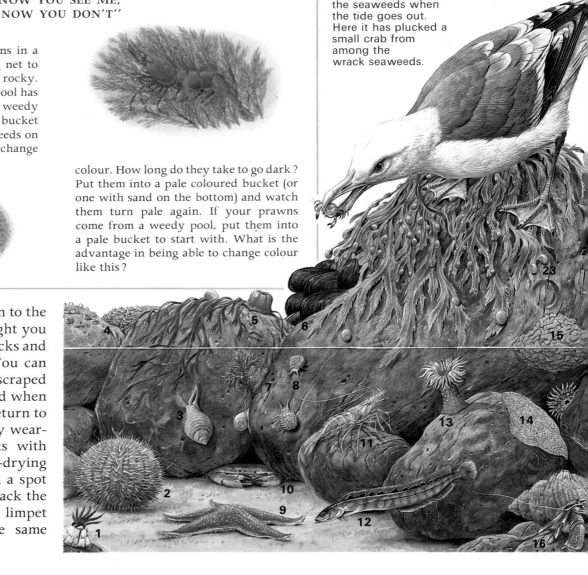

limpets do move: if you go down to the shore when the tide is out at night you will see them gliding over the rocks and browsing on the slimy algae. You can even see tracks where they have scraped the algae away. Limpets also feed when the tide is in, but they always return to the same spot to rest, eventually wearing little grooves in the rocks with their shells. Put a ring of quick-drying paint around a limpet shell and a spot of paint on the shell itself. Go back the next day and you will find the limpet clamped down in exactly the same position.

52

SHELLS OF ALL SHAPES

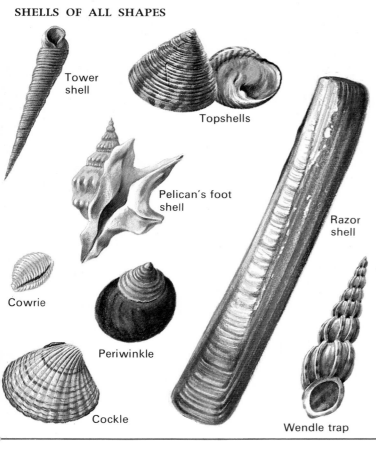

Tower shell

Topshells

Pelican's foot shell

Razor shell

Cowrie

Periwinkle

Cockle

Wendle trap

Left: A selection of sea shells which you can find on various kinds of sea shore. The one-piece spiral or conical shells belong to a group of molluscs called gastropods — the group to which our pond and garden snails belong. Some sea snails, such as the winkles, browse on seaweeds, but others are flesh-eaters. The dog-whelk, for example, can drill right through the shell of another mollusc and suck out the soft body. Cockles, mussels, razor shells, oysters, and scallops are some of the many bivalve molluscs. These have two parts or valves to their shells and the two parts are hinged together along one edge. Look for the horny hinge, and also for the little inter-locking teeth along that edge.

red seaweeds are very delicate and finely branched, and many have 'skeletons' of limestone around them. Seaweeds of this kind help to form coral reefs in tropical seas. If you take these lime-covered plants out of the water and dry them they will lose their red colour and become quite white.

Pool Dwellers

Sea anemones thrive in rock pools because they are always under water and able to feed all the time. Look at their delicate tentacles waving about in the water, like the petals of a flower. One colourful species is actually called the dahlia anemone. But sea anemones are not flowers. They are animals, and carnivorous ones at that. You might be lucky enough to see one catch a shrimp or a small fish. If not, just drop a small piece of meat on to the tentacles of one of them. The tentacles will immediately curl around the meat and push it into the animal's mouth. Live animals are trapped and paralysed by minute stings on the tentacles.

Some of the many kinds of animals that you can find in a rock pool. Try to keep very still while watching a pool, and do not let your shadow fall on to the water, as this might send some of the animals hurrying for cover.

1. Acorn barnacle feeding (notice the feathery limbs)
2. Edible sea urchin
3. Dog whelk
4. Acorn barnacles
5. Beadlet anemone (closed)
6. Mussels
7. Beadlet anemone (open)
8. Topshells
9. Starfish
10. Crab
11. Common prawn
12. Butterfish
13. Anemone
14. Sea squirt colony
15. Whelk egg cases
16. Hermit crab
17. Ragworm
18. Sea slug
19. Tube-worms
20. Goby
21. Brittle star
22. Plumose anemone
23. Periwinkles
24. Limpets

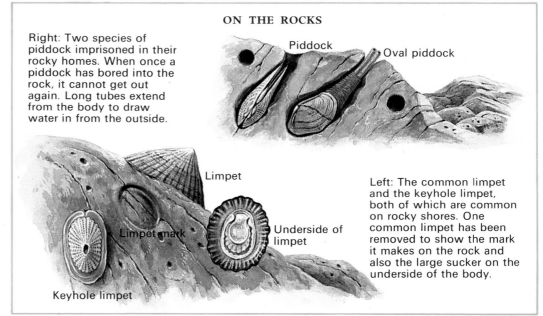

ON THE ROCKS

Right: Two species of piddock imprisoned in their rocky homes. When once a piddock has bored into the rock, it cannot get out again. Long tubes extend from the body to draw water in from the outside.

Piddock

Oval piddock

Limpet

Limpet mark

Keyhole limpet

Underside of limpet

Left: The common limpet and the keyhole limpet, both of which are common on rocky shores. One common limpet has been removed to show the mark it makes on the rock and also the large sucker on the underside of the body.

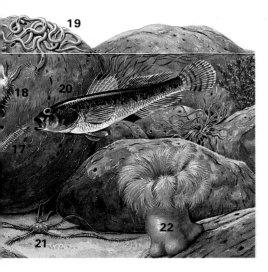

which look like scrawls of white paint. You will also see many little blobs of 'jelly'. These are sea anemones that have pulled all their tentacles in and contracted their bodies to prevent loss of water. To see these beautiful animals properly you need to look in a rock pool.

A Haven in the Rocks

When the tide goes out over a rocky shore quite a lot of water remains behind in rocky hollows. Because there is always some water in these hollows or rock pools, seaweeds, even red ones, can establish themselves. Some of the

Many other animals that would otherwise go out with the tide get trapped in rock pools when the tide is out. The pools thus give you a good opportunity to watch the activities of some of the shallow-water fishes and the shrimps and prawns. You can distinguish shrimps from prawns because prawns have a toothed 'spear' sticking out from the top of the head. Some of these animals are difficult to see because they change their colours to match the background. The chameleon prawn is very good at doing this, and you can watch it change colour in a bucket (see page 52).

Right: An acorn barnacle. The barnacle can close its shell when the tide goes out and survive several hours without water. When the tide returns the animal opens its shell again and 'combs' small particles of food from the water with its feathery limbs. Put some barnacles on stones into a bucket of sea water and see them working for yourself.

Above the highest limits of the tide there is a region known as the splash zone, which regularly receives spray from the waves. There may be a few green seaweeds there, but most of the plants are flowering plants and lichens. The plants must be able to tolerate a high concentration of salt.

Common flowers of the splash zone include hottentot fig (1), thrift (2), sea holly (3), samphire (4), and sea bindweed (5) on the dunes. The puffin (6) nests in burrows on the cliff top, while kittiwakes (7) and guillemots (8) nest on rocky cliff ledges.

Sea lettuce

Sea grass

Bryopsis plumosa

Peacock's tail

camium coccineum

Rhodymenia palmata

Irish moss
or carrageen

Serrated wrack

Oarweed

WEEDS BELOW THE WATER

Seaweeds belong to a group of plants called algae. They have no flowers and they reproduce by scattering minute spores into the water. There are four main groups: the blue-green seaweeds, which are very tiny, the greens, the browns, and the reds. The brown seaweeds are the most abundant on the shore, and they also include the largest seaweeds – the long kelps and oarweeds that form dense 'forests' just below low-tide level. Some are more than 100 metres long. The seaweed below is bladder wrack, a very common brown seaweed on rocky shores, recognised by its many air bladders.

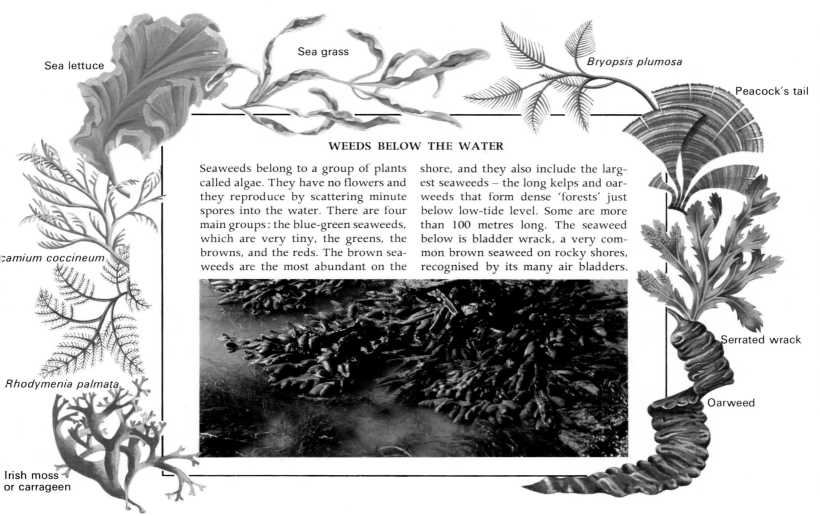

Crabs often hide themselves away in the crevices of a rock pool. There are always more crabs than you can see, and you can tempt them out by taking another small piece of meat. Tie the meat to a piece of string and dangle it in the pool. If there is a crab in residence it may well grab the meat so tightly with one of its great claws that you can lift the whole animal out of the water. Put it on the rocks and watch it move with its curious sideways motion. See its eyes standing out on stalks and its tiny, tweezer-like jaws at the front. The crab uses these to pick up little pieces of food from the sea bed. What do you think the large claws are used for? Most crabs merely walk about on the sea bed, but some can swim. Look at the back legs of crabs, and you will see that some are broad and feathery. These belong to the swimming crabs and they are used as paddles.

You will see lots of seasnails in the pool – animals such as whelks, dogwhelks, periwinkles, and top-shells. Most of them crawl very slowly over the rocks and seaweeds, but do not be surprised to see a shell suddenly dart across the bottom of the pool. Such a fast-moving shell will not, of course, contain a mollusc: it will have been taken over by a hermit crab. Pick up the shell and have a look inside: all you will see are the large claws of the crab blocking the shell entrance. If you put the shell into a bucket of sea water you will see the animal gradually emerge. Watch it put out its feelers or antennae to explore its new surroundings before putting out its legs. The hermit crab will not come right out of the shell because it has a very soft back end and it uses the shell as a portable home. As it gets bigger, the crab searches for larger shells and changes house every now and then. Look for small hermit crabs in winkle shells cast up on the beach, and also on the fishmonger's slab.

A sun-star crawling over seaweeds with the aid of its numerous tube feet, some of which can be seen under the upturned tips of the arms. Most starfishes have just five arms.

Home and High Street

There is much less variety of plant and animal life in built-up areas than in the open country, but do not think that you cannot study nature indoors or in the town. Our homes and other buildings are full of food and other materials useful to animals.

Many animals make a very good living by tagging on to our wasteful communities and clearing up the scraps. Some, notably rats and mice, have become serious pests.

The house sparrow is probably the commonest bird in towns, but you will not find it in the open country. Have a look around you every time you see a house sparrow and you will find that you are almost always within sight of a building of some kind. Try to find out what the birds are eating and where their nests are. Almost all the house sparrow's food consists of materials provided by man. Grain is particularly important to them and they are especially common around farms, docks, and railway yards. Why do you think this is? What do you think might happen to the house sparrow if people disappeared altogether?

Make a list of all the other kinds of birds that you find in the town and try to find out what each kind eats. Starlings are very common birds in towns today and they are often a serious nuisance because they roost on trees and buildings in large numbers and make a mess with their droppings. Try to find a starling roost and see just how many birds there are. The best time to look for them is a winter afternoon.

House Guests

Silverfish, clothes moths, carpet beetles, and woodworm (another little beetle) are just a few of the insects that make themselves at home in houses, even the cleanest and tidiest. Search for these and other insects in your house and draw each kind that you discover. Try to find out what each one eats and whether it does any damage in the house. Many insects eat wool, fur, feathers, and other dried materials. Where do you think these insects lived before people started to build houses? Examine an old bird's nest and you

A cloud of town pigeons (right) rise in front of St Mark's, Venice. Here and in many other towns they live well on scraps and rubbish in the streets, and from the thousands of people who like to feed them. The birds are descended from the wild rock dove, which nests and roosts on cliffs, so the pigeons are quite at home on buildings.

A rubbish bin (bottom) provides a banquet of our leftovers for some unfussy house sparrows and a thrush.

Do not throw away food that has 'gone off' immediately. It is fascinating to watch moulds develop. Notice the tiny pin-like spore capsules on the rotten tomato below.

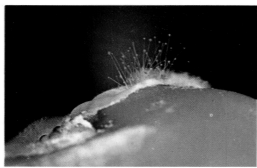

might find the answer to this question.

Look out also for plant guests in the house, such as the moulds that grow on forgotten fruit and bread. Moisten a slice of bread and leave it on a saucer for a few days. Keep it moist, and you will be amazed at how many different kinds of mould develop on it.

Look Where You Walk

Heavily used pavements in the middle of towns are usually quite bare, but suburban pavements and garden paths support a surprising number of small plants in the narrow cracks between the slabs. Most of these plants will be mosses, one of the commonest being the silvery thread moss, so called because of the silvery tinge to the leaves and stems. Take a close look at a piece of this moss and see how the leaves cluster tightly around the stems making them look like short, upright catkins. See also how the stems are packed closely together to form a spongy mass between the paving stones. It is this spongy texture that soaks up water when it rains and helps the moss to survive through the dry weather. The silvery thread moss puts up with air pollution better than any other moss and grows on walls right in the middle

The silverfish is a little wingless insect fond of larders and other dark cupboards. It eats starchy foods.

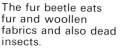
The woolly bear is the larva of the carpet beetle. It chews carpets and other fabrics.

The fur beetle eats fur and woollen fabrics and also dead insects.

The clothes moth does no damage itself, but its caterpillar chews holes in wool.

The furniture beetle, or woodworm grub, tunnels in furniture, floor-boards, and other wood in the house.

The house-fly crawls on dung and on rubbish dumps and then carries germs to our tables.

The blow-fly, or bluebottle, will lay its eggs on any uncovered meat or fish.

of towns. It is rarely found in open country.

A path which is not often used quickly becomes covered with other plants as well as mosses. Small seeds get trapped in the pavement cracks and send up blades of grass and other shoots. See how many different types of plants you can find growing on neglected paths and pavements. A path

Above: Some common household insects.

Left: Winged ants emerging from the ground for their marriage flights.

Left above: The house cricket (top) and the German cockroach like plenty of warmth and are usually found in bakeries and large kitchens, but the others can be found in any house.

WATCH THEM AT WORK

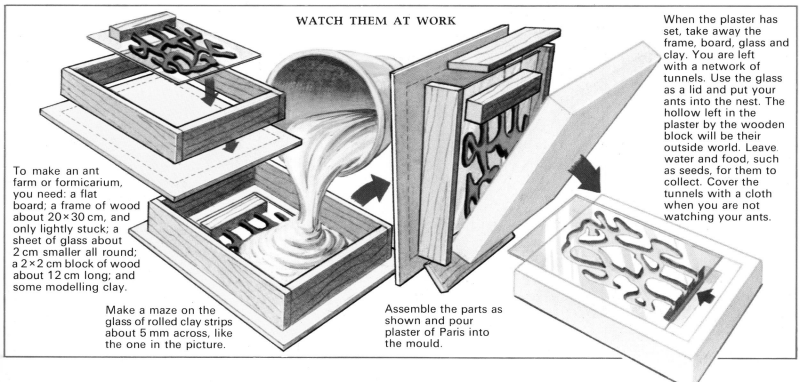

To make an ant farm or formicarium, you need: a flat board; a frame of wood about 20×30 cm, and only lightly stuck; a sheet of glass about 2 cm smaller all round; a 2×2 cm block of wood about 12 cm long; and some modelling clay.

Make a maze on the glass of rolled clay strips about 5 mm across, like the one in the picture.

Assemble the parts as shown and pour plaster of Paris into the mould.

When the plaster has set, take away the frame, board, glass and clay. You are left with a network of tunnels. Use the glass as a lid and put your ants into the nest. The hollow left in the plaster by the wooden block will be their outside world. Leave water and food, such as seeds, for them to collect. Cover the tunnels with a cloth when you are not watching your ants.

which is absolutely abandoned soon becomes completely overgrown. Nettles and brambles spring up in the cracks, and the force of their spreading roots and stems lifts and cracks the slabs. You can see the same thing happen on abandoned tennis courts and railway lines and also on old walls (see below).

Flying Ants

On certain humid days in the summer the air in both town and country may become filled with flying black ants. The ants are on their marriage flights and, if you look at the pavement cracks and garden paths, you will see that the ants are streaming out from the ground over a very large area. All the nests in a town erupt at the same time. The eruption is clearly controlled by the climatic conditions, and it is worth

making a note of the air temperature if you have a thermometer. Is the sky cloudy or clear when the ants take to the wing, and is there any wind? Note the conditions and see if the ants fly in similar conditions next year.

Watch the swallows and house martins swooping to and fro through the ant swarms and filling themselves with the juicy insects. Then imagine how few of the ants ever reach the ground again. Look at the ants that land and you will see that some are much larger than others. The large ones are the females, or queens, whose bodies are full of eggs.

You may see them rubbing themselves against small stones. They do this to break off their wings which they no longer need, for they will spend the rest of their lives underground.

Baby spiders (right) spreading out from their egg cocoon which had been attached to a window sill. Each will soon pull out a silken thread and drift away on it to find a new home, but most will die before they grow up. Wolf spiders (left) can often be seen on the garden path. The female carries her egg cocoon with her, and the young spiders ride on her back for a few days before dispersing.

Old walls and derelict buildings very soon become clothed with plants, whose seeds or spores find the old, loose mortar a good rooting place. After the last war, the bombed sites in London and other towns became extremely colourful as the broken walls and piles of rubble sprouted a wide range of flowering plants. Some of the plants are garden escapees, while others are familiar weeds, but they all arrive on the derelict sites by way of light, wind-blown seeds or by way of various animals (see page 12). Colonisation of waste land and old buildings by plants is all part of the natural process of succession, which we have already seen in the grasslands (page 38) and in the ponds (page 47). It shows that nature is always ready to take over as

Plane trees are often grown in towns to provide shade. They do not seem to be affected by air pollution, perhaps because of the way in which the old bark flakes off (below).

LOPPING THE TOPS

Many suburban and city streets are lined with trees. The trees have to be trimmed regularly because of the traffic. Many are cut right back to the main trunk or branches every year or so, and a dense crop of thin shoots springs up from the cut stumps. The continual cutting back causes the branches to swell up like heads, giving the trees a very unusual look. This process is called pollarding.

If you come across a nest of black ants under a stone, you might like to try transferring them to a formicarium (see page 57). Make sure that you collect the queen – she is much larger than the other ants – if you want the colony to flourish.

Spiders Everywhere

Around your doors and windows you will always find spider webs in summer and autumn. Most of the spiders die as winter approaches, but they leave their eggs, safely wrapped in little balls of silk. Look for these in the corners of window frames and under the sills. Leave them alone, and you will be able to watch the hundreds of tiny spiders emerging from them in the spring (see picture). Look for wolf spiders running over the paths and for the little black and white zebra spider scurrying about on old walls. You might see it jump on a fly.

Down The High Street

Shops provide plenty of interest for the naturalist. While queuing in the greengrocer's, see how many different kinds of fruits and vegetables you can spot. Look at the variety of fishes and other sea creatures on the fishmonger's slab, and watch the wasps buzzing round the cakes in the baker's. At night, the shops' lights often attract moths for you to look at. Even in the winter you can find moths on the shop windows, but a cold winter evening is probably best spent with a good natural history book. You will then be able to appreciate nature all around you even better the following year.

LICHENS LIKE WALLS

Old walls and asbestos roofs are often clothed with colourful lichens. These are strange plants, each consisting of a mixture of a fungus and an alga (a simple relative of the seaweeds). They are very hardy and they can grow on dry walls in the full sun, but they do not like air pollution. See how much more common they are in suburban and country areas than in the town centre. A good place to look for them is on old gravestones in a cemetery. You can also find them on tree trunks.

soon as we relax our grip and stop doing the weeding. Left completely alone, even a derelict building site would be converted into a small wood, with the trees gradually breaking down all the buildings with the power of their roots. The picture here shows a number of common plants which you can expect to find on and around old walls. They are, from left to right: rosebay willowherb, wall rue fern, herb robert, ivy-leaved toadflax, yellow corydalis, annual meadow grass (on top of wall), navelwort, Oxford ragwort (on pavement), annual wall rocket, wallflower, and wild chamomile (on pavement). Wall screw moss can also be seen on the wall, while the silvery thread moss is growing well on the broken pavement.

CLUBS TO JOIN

Amateur Entomologists' Society
23 Manor Way, North Harrow, Middlesex
The society has a flourishing junior section and deals with insects of all kinds

British Naturalists' Association
Willowfield, Boyneswood Road, Four Marks, Alton, Hants

British Trust for Conservation Volunteers
c/o Zoological Gardens, Regents Park, London NW1
The trust organises work camps to carry out maintenance work on nature reserves, but you must be 16 years old before you can join

Field Studies Council
Preston Montford, Montford Bridge, Shrewsbury
The council organises field courses in all branches of natural history, some courses being designed mainly for younger people

Wildlife Youth Service
Marston Court, 98–106 Manor Road, Wallington, Surrey
WYS is the junior branch of the World Wildlife Fund, concerned with the conservation of the world's wild animals and plants

Young Ornithologists' Club (YOC)
The Lodge, Sandy, Bedfordshire
YOC is the junior branch of the Royal Society for the Protection of Birds. It organises projects and field trips

Young Zoologists' Club (XYZ Club)
c/o The London Zoo, Regents Park, London, NW1
The club encourages children to take an interest in wild animals of all kinds

Your local natural history society is also well worth joining. As a member, you may be able to go on excursions to see the countryside and you will also be able to meet other people with similar interests. There is also a Naturalists' Trust covering your own county or area. The trusts own a number of nature reserves, which members can visit to see rare plants and animals. The addresses of your local trust or natural history society can be obtained from your local library or else from the Council for Nature, *c/o Zoological Gardens, Regents Park, London, NW1.*

BOOKS TO READ

Most of the books listed below will help you to identify some of the plants and animals that you find in your garden or in the countryside.

Observer Books, published by Frederick Warne
These inexpensive books, well illustrated in colour, deal with a wide range of natural history subjects, such as grasses, mosses, fishes, and birds

Wayside and Woodland Books, published by Frederick Warne, cover many groups of plants and animals in more detail than the Observer books.
Useful titles include:
Wayside and Woodland Ferns, by E. Step
Wayside and Woodland Blossoms by E. Step (3 volumes)
Wayside and Woodland Trees by H. L. Edlin
The Freshwater Life of the British Isles by J. Clegg
British Shells by N. F. McMillan
Land and Water Bugs of the British Isles by Southwood and Leston
Beetles of the British Isles by E. F. Linssen (2 volumes)
Grasshoppers, Crickets and Cockroaches of the British Isles, by D. R. Ragge
Flies of the British Isles by Colyer and Hammond
The Moths of the British Isles by R. South (2 volumes)
The Caterpillars of British Moths by W. J. Stokoe (2 volumes)
The Butterflies of the British Isles by R. South
The Caterpillars of the British Butterflies by W. J. Stokoe

Clue Books, published by Oxford University Press, contain simple, but very useful keys for the identification of plants and animals. Titles include:
Birds, Flowers, Insects, Freshwater Animals, Seashore Animals, Flowerless Plants, and Trees

Collins Field Guides cover a wide range of subjects. Some of the most useful titles include:
The Wild Flowers of Britain and Northern Europe by Fitter, Fitter and Blamey

Trees of Britain and Northern Europe by A. Mitchell
Mammals of Britain and Europe by F. H. van den Brink
Insects of Britain and Northern Europe by M. Chinery
Butterflies of Britain and Europe by Higgins and Riley
Birds of Britain and Europe by Heinzel, Fitter, and Parslow
Mushrooms and Toadstools by Lange and Hora
Animals Tracks and Signs by Bang and Dahlstrom
Freshwater Fishes of Britain and Europe by Muus and Dahlstrom
Pocket Guide to the Seashore by Barrett and Yonge
A Guide to the British Landscape by J. R. W. Cheatle

Other useful books for the young naturalist include:
The Natural History of the Garden by M. Chinery (Collins)
Discovering Garden Insects and other Invertebrates by A. Wootton (Shire)
The Insects in Your Garden by H. Oldroyd
Marine Life by de Haas and Knoor (Burke)
Pond Life by W. Engelhardt (Burke)
Molluscs by H. Janus (Burke)
Animal Life in Fresh Water by H. Mellanby (Methuen)
Plant Galls in Colour by A. Darlington (Blandford)
The Ecology of Towns by A. Leutscher (Watts)
The New Bird Table Book by Tony Soper (David & Charles)
Pleasure from Insects by M. Tweedie (David & Charles)
Guide to Watching Wildlife by D. Stephen (Collins)
The Concise British Flora in Colour by Keble Martin (Michael Joseph)
The Field by L. Jackman (Evans)
Exploring the Hedgerows by L. Jackman (Evans)
Exploring the Park by L. Jackman (Evans)
Exploring the Seashore by L. Jackman (Evans)
Exploring the Woodland by L. Jackman (Evans)
Nature Through the Seasons by Adams and Hooper (Penguin)

ACKNOWLEDGMENTS

The publishers are greatly indebted to the author for his kindness in providing the majority of photographs in this book. The remaining photographs were kindly supplied by: Heather Angel (Endpapers & pp 18 bottom, 19 top, 40 top, 41 right and 54); Pat Morris (pp 56 bottom, 57 centre, and 59 left); NHPA (pp 13, 16, 24 top, 26 centre right, 29 left, and 37); ZEFA (pp 10, 34, 35 top, 43, 56 top, and 58 right).

Index

Numerals in *italics* indicate illustrations